ALLEN COUNTY PUBLIC LIBRARY

FORT WAYNE, INDIANA 46802

You may return this book to any agency, branch,
or bookmobile of the Allen County Public Library.

The Deficits:
How Big? How Long?
How Dangerous?

THE JOSEPH I. LUBIN MEMORIAL LECTURES

NUMBER 2

Daniel Bell

Henry Ford II
Professor of Social Sciences
Harvard University

Lester Thurow

Gordon Y. Billard
Professor of Economics and Management
Massachusetts Institute of Technology

The Deficits:
How Big? How Long?
How Dangerous?

The Joseph I. Lubin Memorial Lectures
College of Business and Public Administration
New York University

NEW YORK UNIVERSITY PRESS
NEW YORK AND LONDON
1985

Library of Congress Cataloging in Publication Data

Bell, Daniel.
  The deficits : how big? how long? how dangerous?

  (Joseph I. Lubin memorial lectures : 2)
  1. Budget deficits—United States—Addresses,
essays, lectures. I. Thurow, Lester C. C. II. Title.
III. Series.
HJ2051.B45 1985   339.5′23′0973   85-13568
ISBN 0-8147-1083-2

c 10 9 8 7 6 5 4 3 2

7103153

FOREWORD

This volume, the second in the Joseph I. Lubin Memorial Lectures series, which succeeded the Charles C. Moskowitz Memorial Lectures series, is concerned with a topic which continues to command the attention of almost everyone, for the problem it concerns simply will not go away. That topic is the National deficit: *How Big? How Long? How Dangerous?* Actually, the questions posed by the topic are, at least in their simplest form, somewhat rhetorical and disingenuous. We all know the deficits are big, will extend over a period of years, and are dangerous to our own and perhaps the world's long-run well-being. There appears to be a consensus among almost all knowledgeable observers and commentators that corrective actions will have to be taken and that those actions will necessarily and unavoidably involve taxes, spending on social programs, and spending on military programs.

One could well ask: With so much agreement, what's the problem? That question, too, is rhetorical and disingenuous, because the problem is one of values and priorities, and on those things there is great disagreement. In fact, one may fairly wonder about the capacity of a political democracy like our own to resolve the problem. We must hope that there will be a general understanding that failure to achieve a resolution will carry long-run dangers, and even terrors, if we look to the history and the fate of other nations. With that problem as a backdrop we asked two of our nation's leading thinkers and commentators, Dr. Daniel Bell and Dr. Lester Thurow, to address the topic of this year's Lubin lectures.

Dr. Bell is New York born and bred, having graduated from Stuyvesant High School, City College, and Columbia University. After a long and distinguished career as a writer and editor with several of our country's best-known magazines, he joined the ranks of academicians as a professor of sociology, first at Columbia and then at Harvard. Today, he is the Henry Ford II Professor of Social Sciences at Harvard. The author of many books and the recipient of many honors, Dr. Bell has served on a number of presidential commissions. A cofounder and coeditor of the influential journal the *Public Interest,* he is today also on the board of editors of *Daedalus* and a contributing editor to *Partisan Review.*

Daniel Bell's paper sees our federal deficits as caught up in and confounded by the political forces emanating from a variety of pressure groups. The middle class, which he describes as now outnumbering the have-nots in our society, is the major beneficiary of the 1981 tax reductions; it is unlikely to support tax increases. It is also a substantial beneficiary of Social Security and Medicare. Defense expenditures appear to be beyond really significant cuts, and expenditures for social programs other than Social Security and Medicare are insufficient in magnitude to offer a solution through their being slashed. On top of this the overhanging threat of the structural deficit looms ever larger as one faces the future.

Bell does not offer a "solution." Rather, he describes the degree to which an economic problem has been politicized, or and even "idiologized."

Any solution would thus appear to depend on a reduction in the level of heat and passion and in the emergence of a social decision which overrides narrower and more limited interests.

The second Lubin lecturer, Dr. Lester Thurow, was born in Livingston, Montana and educated at Williams College, Balliol College at Oxford University, where he was a Rhodes Scholar, and Harvard University. Still a young man, Dr. Thurow has already had a most distinguished career as an academician, being presently Gordon Y. Billard professor of economics and management at the Massachusetts Institute of Technology. He has also been most active as an editor and economic consultant to many of the nation's leading newspapers and magazines, as well as a member of important national commissions. An extraordinarily prolific writer, his work has appeared in learned journals, as well as in magazines and newspapers. His writings are much more than a testimonial to his youth and energy, for those qualities relate only to his volume of output. The fact is that his volume of output is a response to an insatiable demand for the benefit of his judgment and opinion.

While Thurow agrees with Bell that overcoming the deficit problem requires its depoliticization, which is unsure, he differs greatly in his readiness to provide specific prescriptions. Before getting to those prescriptions he points out four major problems which derive from massive deficits: (1) reduced investment and lower productivity; (2) increased inflationary pressures; (3) a diminished capacity to fight future recessions; and (4) reduced international competitiveness. To those who argue that the deficits are not serious he figuratively gives the back of his hand.

Turning to specifics, Thurow calls for major changes in our taxing and expenditure policies. In the former connection he would (1) eliminate the personal and corporate income taxes; (2) reduce indirect business and social insurance taxes; (3) introduce a personal consumption tax and a value-added tax; and (4) increase the excise tax on gasoline (by $1 per gallon). He sees these measures as producing a far more equitable tax system, which would have such enormously beneficial attributes as increasing saving and investment, dealing a body blow to the underground economy, and enhancing our society's productiveness and international competitiveness.

In connection with expenditures, Thurow focuses on defense, the elderly, and health care. Defense, he says, must get what is necessary for our collective security. However, the burden of the defense of the free world can no longer be disproportionately carried by the United States. Our allies have, after all, long since recovered from the devastation of World War II, and their ability to pay a larger share of the burden of our muual defense has been greatly increased. As to the elderly, Thurow notes that they are now somewhat better off economically than younger people. Since the issue here involves distribution of society's output among the various generations, equity is needed, not favoritism on either side. With respect to health care, Thurow points out that it must be curbed at a level which society can afford, a level which it has probably been outstripping. Of course, a profound ethical issue is involved. That is, how do we say no to someone whose life would be marginally increased by a very costly treatment which simply cannot be provided to everyone? We must find an answer to that question.

Finally, this reminder is appropriate. Both lecturers see no solution to the decrease in the national debt unless we depoliticize the deficit problem. If we fail to do so, then we are in for a future crisis the outcome of which is alarming.

Appreciation is due to my assistants, Virginia Moress and Amanda Sherman, as well as to my secretary, Eileen Cassidy. As always, professors Ernest Bloch and Ernest Kurnow, the members of the advisory committee on the Lubin lectures, were most helpful. And I am grateful to the staff of the NYU Press for their never flagging efforts in producing this volume.

Abraham L. Gitlow

January 8, 1985

Dean, College of Business and Public Administration

THE JOSEPH I. LUBIN
MEMORIAL LECTURES

THE JOSEPH I. LUBIN MEMORIAL LECTURES were established through the generosity of a distinguished trustee of New York University, the late Joseph I. Lubin. Mr. Lubin, who was a preeminent force in the business and philanthropic community, wished to provide a public forum for the discussion and practical application of economic and management theories.

This extraordinary humanitarian will also be remembered for his civic and philanthropic endeavors. In addition to New York University's Eisner & Lubin Auditorium, he has enriched this city by his contributions of the Joseph I. Lubin Pace Schools of Business, the Joseph I. Lubin Syracuse House, and the Evelyn J. and Joseph I. Lubin Rehabilitation Center and Center for Learning Disabilities at the Albert Einstein College of Medicine. Mr. Lubin was a Gallatin Fellow and a Haskins Associate of this university. He also served as a trustee of Syracuse and Pace Universities and of the Albert Einstein College of Medicine.

This volume is the second in the Joseph I. Lubin Memorial Lecture series and is modeled after our past distinguished Charles C. Moskowitz Memorial Lecture Series. A complete listing of these lectures can be found on the following pages.

February, 1961   *Business Survival in the Sixties*
                      Thomas F. Patton, President and Chief Executive Officer
                      Republic Steel Corporation

November, 1961   *The Challenges Facing Management*
                      Don G. Mitchell, President
                      General Telephone and Electronics Corporation

November, 1962   *Competitive Private Enterprise Under Government Regulation*
                      Malcolm A. MacIntyre, President
                      Eastern Air Lines

November, 1963   *The Common Market: Friend or Competitor?*
                      Jesse W. Markham, Professor of Economics, Princeton University
                      Charles E. Fiero, Vice President, The Chase Manhattan Bank
                      Howard S. Piquet, Senior Specialist in International Economics, Legislative Reference Service, The Library of Congress

November, 1964   *The Forces Influencing the American Economy*
                      Jules Backman, Research Professor of Economics, New York University
                      Martin R. Gainsbrugh, Chief Economist and Vice President, National Industrial Conference Board

November, 1965   *The American Market of the Future*
                      Arno H. Johnson, Vice President and Senior Economist, J. Walter Thompson Company

Gilbert E. Jones, President, IBM World Trade Corporation

Darrell B. Lucas, Professor of Marketing and Chairman of the Department, New York University

November, 1966   *Government Wage-Price Guideposts in the American Economy*

George Meany, President, American Federation of Labor and Congress of Industrial Organizations

Roger M. Blough, Chairman of the Board and Chief Executive Officer, United States Steel Corporation

Neil H. Jacoby, Dean, Graduate School of Business Administration, University of California at Los Angeles

November, 1967   *The Defense Sector in the American Economy*

Jacob J. Javits, United States Senator, New York

Charles J. Hitch, President, University of California

Arthur F. Burns, Chairman, Federal Reserve Board

November, 1968   *The Urban Environment: How It Can Be Improved*

William E. Zisch, Vice-chairman of the Board, Aerojet-General Corporation

Paul H. Douglas, Chairman, National Commission on Urban Problems

Professor of Economics, New School for Social Research

Robert C. Weaver, President, Bernard M. Baruch College of the City University of New York

Former Secretary of Housing and Urban Development

November, 1969   *Inflation: The Problem It Creates and the Policies It Requires*

Arthur M. Okun, Senior Fellow, The Brookings Institution

Henry H. Fowler, General Partner, Goldman, Sachs & Co.

Milton Gilbert, Economic Adviser, Bank for International Settlements

March, 1971   *The Economics of Pollution* .

Kenneth E. Boulding, Professor of Economics, University of Colorado

Elvis J. Stahr, President, National Audubon Society

Solomon Fabricant, Professor of Economics, New York University

Former Director, National Bureau of Economic Research

Martin R. Gainsbrugh, Adjunct Professor of Economics, New York University

Chief Economist, National Industrial Conference Board

April, 1971   *Young America in the NOW World*

Hubert H. Humphrey, Senator from Minnesota

Former Vice President of the United States

April, 1972   *Optimum Social Welfare and Productivity: A Comparative View*

Jan Tinbergen, Professor of Development Planning, Netherlands School of Economics, Nobel Laureate

Abram Bergson, George E. Baker Professor of Economics, Harvard University

Fritz Machlup, Professor of Economics, New York University

April, 1973   *Fiscal Responsibility: Tax Increases or Spending Cuts?*

Paul McCracken, Edmund Ezra Day University, Professor of Business Administration, University of Michigan

Murray L. Weidenbaum, Edward Mallinckrodt Distinguished University Professor, Washington University

Lawrence S. Ritter, Professor of Finance, New York University

Robert A. Kavesh, Professor of Finance, New York University

March, 1974   *Wall Street in Transition: The Emerging System and its Impact on the Economy*

Henry G. Manne, Distinguished Professor of Law, Director of the Center for Studies in Law and Economics, University of Miami Law School

Ezra Solomon, Dean Witter Professor of Finance, Stanford University

March, 1975   *Leaders and Followers in an Age of Ambiguity*
                   George P. Schultz, Professor, Graduate School
                        of Business, Stanford University
                   President, Bechtel Corporation

March, 1976   *The Economic System in an Age of Discontinu-*
                        ity: Long-Range Planning or Market Reli-
                        ance?
                   Wassily Leontief, Nobel Laureate, Professor of
                        Economics, New York University
                   Herbert Stein, A. Willis Robertson Professor of
                        Economics, University of Virginia

March, 1977   *Demographic Dynamics in America*
                   Wilber J. Cohen, Dean of the School of Edu-
                        cation and Professor of Education and of
                        Public Welfare Administration, University of
                        Michigan
                   Charles F. Westhoff, Director of the Office of
                        Population Research and Maurice During
                        Professor of Demographic Studies, Princeton
                        University

March, 1978   *The Rediscovery of the Business Cycle*
                   Paul A. Volcker, President and Chief Executive
                        Officer, Federal Reserve Bank of New York

March, 1979   *Economic Pressure and the Future of The Arts*
                   William Schuman, Composer
                   Roger L. Stevens, Chairman of the Board of
                        Trustees, John F. Kennedy Center for the
                        Performing Arts

April, 1980   *Presidential Promises and Performance*
                     McGeorge Bundy, Professor of History, Faculty
                        of Arts and Science, New York University
                     Edmund S. Muskie, Former U.S. Senator from
                        Maine, Secretary of State

March, 1981   *Econometric Models as Guides for Decision-*
                        Making
                     Lawrence R. Klein, Benjamin Franklin Profes-
                        sor of Finance and Economics, University of
                        Pennsylvania, Nobel Laureate

March, 1982   *The American Economy, 1960–2000*
                     Richard M. Cyert, President, Carnegie–Mellon
                        University

December, 1983   *Reaganomics: Meaning, Means and Ends*
                     John Kenneth Galbraith, Paul M. Warburg Pro-
                        fessor of Economics Emeritus, Harvard Uni-
                        versity
                     Paul W. McCracken, Edmund Ezra Day Distin-
                        guished University Professor of Business Ad-
                        ministration, The University of Michigan, and
                        Chairman, Council of Economic Advisers,
                        American Institute for Public Policy Research

Note: All but the last seven volumes of The Charles C. Moskowitz
      Memorial Lectures were published by the New York Univer-
      sity Press. The 1977, 1978, 1979, 1980, 1981, 1982 and 1983
      lectures were published by The Free Press.

THE JOSEPH I. LUBIN
MEMORIAL LECTURES

March, 1984   *The World Banking System; Outlook in a Context of Crisis*

Andrew F. Brimmer, President of Brimmer & Company Inc. and Chairman of the Monetary Policy Forum

December, 1984   *The Deficits: How Big? How Long? How Dangerous?*

Daniel Bell, Henry Ford II Professor of Social Sciences, Harvard University

Lester Thurow, Gordon Y. Billard Professor of Economics and Management, Massachusetts Institute of Technology

CONTENTS

THROUGH THE LOOKING GLASS: THE BUDGET DEBATE AND THE AMERICAN POLITY, 1984

Daniel Bell
Henry Ford II Professor of Social Sciences
Harvard University

I. Behind the Looking Glass

The sun was shining on the sea,
Shining with all his might:
He did his very best to make
The billows smooth and bright—
And this was odd, because it was
The middle of the night.

If, like Alice, we step through the looking glass, any-
one with a slight historical memory—and how short
memories are, these days of kaleidoscopic political crises;
but, say a memory of 12 years in U.S. electoral history—would have great difficulty (unless we were like
Alice, who, in her supreme common sense and skepti-
cism, was never astounded), in differentiating between
Tweedledum and Twaddledee.

We step back, to 1972. Mr. Nixondum speaks for fiscal responsibility, balanced budgets, and against exces-

27

sive spending. He is, like any traditional Tweedle, a conventional Republican. Mr. McGoverndee is for the expansion of federal programs, especially for the poor; more aid to states and cities; the recognition of minority sexual rights ("gays" and "lesbians"). He is against "the interests." Like so many of the Twaddles, he is, proudly, a "populist."

We return through the time warp. It is now 1984. For almost two years, America has had a deep recession, engineered by a Scrooge-like monetary policy, yet, *mirabile dictu,* a sensational two-year, demand-led recovery, stimulated by what *The Economist* has called "turbocharged Keynesianism," resulting in the largest budget deficits in the U.S. history. Mr. Reagandee strongly defends the tax cuts by which the boom was fuelled, and regards the deficit as an irritating by-product but not a serious problem if his further policies (but no prescriptions are given)—mild tax reform (unspecified) and expansive economic growth—continue. Trust me, says Mr. Reagandee. If I cannot tell you exactly what we plan to do, regard my charmed quark life; it will continue.

Stolid, serious, minatory, Mr. Mondaledum warns that the mundane day of reckoning is to come, that the deficit must be reduced soon, and that the immediate way of doing so is to increase taxes, by at least $85 billion. To refute the Republicans' charge that he intends to tax more only to spend more, Mr. Mondale proposes to set up a deficit-reduction trust fund. By law, every penny of new revenues would go into that fund and be used only for reducing the deficit.

Mr. Reagandee, with the sleight of the illusionist's wand, has borrowed his way into prosperity. Mr. Mondale, strict son of a Lutheran minister, seeks to enforce fiscal probity: Neither a borrower nor a lender be, for the lending bank may have to be bailed out, and the borrower go bankrupt.

Through the looking glass, we may also note with fascination the process of public education. Looking right through the glass, Mr. Reagandee and Mr. Mondaledum give us two-minute simplified disquisitions each on the arcane accounting problems of social-security trust funds as distinct from general funds, on fiscal-year projections of the budget (which do not match calendar years), only to have the two protagonists cut off in their expositions by the warning signals of the moderator. What wonderful compressions of textbook economics! No wonder 85 million watching Americans are mesmerized. Here, truly, is a textbook lesson of the marginal utility of time and the diminishing returns of information.

Since we are still on the other side of the historical looking glass, there persist eerie shadows of the past: Franklin D. Roosevelt, in 1932, running on a platform of balancing the budget, but soon after discovering the compounded magic of the primed pump. Lyndon Johnson, fearing to ask for more taxes to pay for the morally ambiguous war he will be expanding, increases the borrowing, monetarizes the costs, and thus creates inflation which we are just now eliminating from the economy. The fiscal past hovers over all of this still, and the two contendors invoke the litany of exorcism.

Through the refraction of the mirror, we see Mr. Mondale making a determined effort to stake out the center by establishing himself as a fiscal conservative. Yet his realistic political base is made up of the labor unions, the blacks (and, theoretically, the poor and the elderly), all of whom are committed by the nature of their interests and the logic of their positions to an expanded role of government. Mr. Reagan finds his support (foreign policy and cultural issues apart) in the business community, and the *embourgeoisé* blue-collar worker. Yet the business community overwhelmingly dreads the deficit.[1] The market is spooked by the fear of a resurgent inflation.[2] Blue-collar employment in the U.S. is shrinking rapidly.

Mr. Reagan, for one, blithely ignores those fears. When the 1984 *Annual Report of the Council of Economic Advisers,* written by Martin Feldstein, warned that budget deficits will remain high as a "structural fact" of the economy, and that in the next years the need to pay for that deficit would crowd out private investment, the Secretary of the Treasury tells the Congress to "throw away" the report. (And the presidential press spokesman, Larry Speakes, in a calculated putdown, remarks to the White House press corps that he does not know whether the C.E.A. chairman's name is pronounced "Feld-steen" or "Feld-stine.")

Furthermore, when, on July 18, 1984, President Reagan signed the Deficit Reduction Act of 1984, raising taxes by about $50 billion and reducing spending by $13 billion through 1987—the first "down payment" toward reducing the deficit that the Congress and the Administration finally agreed upon—the bill was signed quietly in the Oval Office, at ten o'clock in the morning, with only staff members present. "Larry Speakes, the White House spokesman, said he did not know why there was no ceremony for so significant a piece of legislation," *The New York Times* reported. Does Mr. Reagan "truly" believe that there is no connection between the deficit and the interest rate? As Herbert Stein asks, in his book *Presidential Economics* "If the most 'conservative' President in 50 years would not make any sacrifice in order to avoid the biggest deficit in history, who would?"[3]

And yet, with respect to the electoral events, such

questions as those expressed above are immaterial, if not naïve. Mr. Reagan's *political* strategy has been clear. He bet that America's economic recovery would last through the election without higher interest rates or inflation, or the collapse of the overvalued dollar. And Mr. Reagan's pollsters believe—and most political scientists agree— that, exceptional circumstances apart, the electoral choices in Western societies are heavily determined by economic conditions. As S. M. Lipset remarks: ". . . voters are disposed to credit or blame incumbent administrations for the state of the economy."[4]

One may argue that Mr. Carter bore the burden of an oil shock that quadrupled energy prices and unfavorable farm conditions that sent food prices soaring, and that these were not within his control. And one may argue, conversely, that Mr. Reagan has been the beneficiary of stable and even falling energy prices (of oil and natural gas) and of large food surpluses; and that these were not due to his ministrations. The electorate, however, hearing only two-minute, arcane disquisitions, is not predisposed to listen nor, if listening, to understand. The state of the economy, or the "misery index," is the telltale fulcrum of votes. And so Mr. Reagan, in his electoral statements, has waffled (even when the Republican platform has sought to pin him down, like a butterfly) on the question of tax increases, or how to deal with the budget deficit.

Yet there is the day after election. None of the statements made before that day can whisk the issues away, like the grin of the Cheshire cat. Reality has the awkward habit of splintering a looking glass. A number of difficult questions remain.

There are immediate questions. How serious is the deficit issue? Can we agree on the facts? If we make different assumptions about the level of the deficit, what are the constraints and the options in the policy choices to be made?

Every one of these questions raises other, larger and more-troublesome questions about the way policy is made and the alignments in politics today. I will speak to three:

1. How adequate is the nature of economic advice and the economic data on which different assumptions are made? Is it "only" that Keynesian and monetarist views are outmoded, to be replaced, say, by a more adequate "rational-expectations" approach, or is it, to use a quick shorthand, that the "exogenous" factors of reality are swamping our econometric models, and that economic theory has been cut adrift, buffeted by political tides on some uncharted seas? In sum: Is the problem the growing inadequacy of "economic science" and our misplaced hopes in fine tuning, or not?

2. Are we witnessing the breakup of a political consensus? Is there a new change in the American polity— one that has been predicted by Walter Dean Burnham and Kevin Phillips for almost 20 years? Or are we witnessing what Lipset has argued is the "normal" change in support for the "ins" and "outs," shifting with good times and bad times?

3. What is the meaning of the new "populism," now centered largely on the right, rather than, paradoxically, on the left, as it was historically, and the strong salience of emotional "cultural" or "symbolic" issues? Is this a new politics, and if so, how does it relate to economic alignments and to electoral support?

And behind these are the larger philosophical questions about the continuity and character of American society.

1. What is the proper role of government in a dem-

ocratic society? Is it primarily to foster the initiative, self-interest, and wealth-seeking purposes of individuals and enterprises, or does the concept of citizenship put the idea of community, and the inclusion of the disadvantaged and dispossessed, as the primary lien on resources, economic and educational?

2. What is the future of democracy, then, in a mass society where party systems are breaking down, when plebiscetarian actions, such as referenda, begin to constrain and shape economic policy, and when a philosophy is voiced by a president who tells the people that they should not trust government?

3. How does one deal with the structural problems of managing the transition from the old industrial economy to a new postindustrial, high-tech, or information society (call it what you will)? While the nomenclature may be ambiguous, the facts and direction of change are not.

4. How does one manage a political state (large as ours is) in an interdependent world economy whose very structure (such as the globalization of capital markets) now erases political boundaries? To restate a question I asked a number of years ago: Has the national state become too small for the big problems of life and too big for the small problems of life?[5]

II. Benchmarks

Now, here, you see, it takes all the running you can do to stay in the same place. If you want to get somewhere else, you must run at least twice as fast as that.

We have been dallying with the rhetoric of whimsy, but sometimes play has to be put aside. In this section we shall present stern facts, for only if we have these facts—and agree upon them—can we begin to answer the more-difficult questions about the choices we can make and the policies we might wish to pursue.

In 1981–1982 the United States experienced one of the deepest recessions in its history. Then, it saw one of the sharpest recoveries. In 1982 about 7.5 percent of the labor force was unemployed; at one point, this climbed to 11 percent unemployed; today we are back to about 7.7 percent unemployed. And yet 20 million new jobs have also been created, not just in the dominant service sector, which has been, extraordinarily, almost recession proof, but in manufacturing jobs as well. More than half of these new jobs, however, are held by women, so that the average wage level has dropped somewhat.

The gross national product, which had fallen by 0.3 percent in 1980, one of the first negative figures in postwar economic history, grew by about 6 percent in 1984. Inflation, which was running at about 12.5 percent in 1980, was down to 4 percent in 1984. The prime rate of interest which had reached as high as 20 percent in 1980, were down to about 12.5 percent in 1984. For the consumer, the drop in prices due to the decrease in inflation was substantial. For the businessman, the home buyer, those borrowers requiring credit and working capital, the costs of money, however, was about the same.

The budget is the fulcrum of Federal economic policy. For the first three fiscal years of Mr. Reagan's administration, through 1984, the Congress authorized spending of $2.37 trillion. True, the administration would have spent the money somewhat differently; it would have expended larger amounts for defense and smaller amounts for social programs. But in calculating the deficit, allocations of money are less relevant. The difference between Mr. Reagan's total spending proposals and the budgets passed by Congress was, over three years, a minute $26 billion, or about one-twentieth of the almost $480 billion federal deficit during that period.[6] Federal budget spending, as a share of the gross national product, went from 23.5 percent in fiscal 1981 to 23.9 percent in fiscal 1985.

Mr. Reagan had promised to balance the budget in three years. By the end of four fiscal years the amassed deficits were $650 billion, or the equal of the cumulative deficit totals incurred from Franklin D. Roosevelt to Jimmy Carter. The deficit had been $59 billion in the last Carter year. It was $175 billion in the fiscal year ending September 30. From 1948 to 1980, the total federal debt grew at a slower rate than the gross national product. In 1980, the trend was reversed completely. The *publicly* held federal debt is now at $1.3 trillion, or 35.4 percent of GNP. It is projected, by the Congressional Budget Office, nearly to double to $2.5 trillion in 1989, or 46 percent of GNP. Interest payments, as a percentage of total budget outlays, now about 13.1 percent in fiscal 1984, are projected to rise to 16.4 percent in 1989.

Projections, of course, are chancy. They depend on a number of variables, such as the level of the interest rate (a key element in the costs of servicing the debt); the level of inflation, as a register of prices; and the degree of employment and economic growth. The administration believes that the budget deficits will be decreased substantially in the next five years, on the basis of three assumptions: a 4 percent annual growth rate; a 4 to 4.5 percent inflation; a rate of federal spending increases of 5 percent. The Congressional Budget Office—in estimates made by Rudolph Penner, a conservative and former fellow of the American Enterprise Institute—assumes a 3 percent growth rate for the next five-year period. Whatever the nuances of difference (and 1 percent can be substantial), both assume that after three years of growth, there will be five more years without a recession, or, if there is a recession, a recovery strong enough to overcome the dip in growth within that period.

To sum up, the positive results of the years after 1980 have included a strong recovery, about 20 million new jobs, and a 4 percent inflation rate. How was all this done? One can—the influence of falling energy and food prices apart—identify three reasons.

For one reason, there was the remarkable coincidence of Mr. Reagan's *fiscal* stimulus and Mr. Paul Volcker's *monetary* restraint. Throughout all the years during which Keynesian economics has prevailed and when wage-price bargains or government fiscal actions pumped up the price levels, monetary authorities would respond by increasing the monetary supply. This is what happened in the United States and the United Kingdom in the 1960s and 1970s. Mr. Volcker, to the contrary, maintained his independence. As he once put it: "If we don't tell them how to run fiscal policy, they won't tell us how to run monetary policy." This extraordinary application of fiscal expansion and monetary tightness kept spending high, inflation low, and interest rates high, without the entire economy going through the roof.

A second reason was that the extraordinary government borrowing did not crowd out private investment. This was due to the fact that, because of high interest rates and a strong dollar, there were huge foreign capital inflows of between $80 to 90 billion, or about 25 percent of America's net savings. Directly or indirectly, Paul Volcker told the Congress in July 1984, we are financing our budget deficit from abroad.

The third reason was the remarkable degree of wage restraint. Through the 1970s, as Assar Lindbeck at Stockholm University and Jeffrey Sachs at Harvard University have demonstrated, the sharp increases in real wage rates far above full-employment labor productivity (about 7 to 8 percent in the major O.E.C.D. countries), superimposed on historically low and even negative interest rates and returns, created a wage-push inflation which almost everywhere was accommodated by the monetary authorities.[7] Today that wage-push spiral has been ended. In the United States in 1981, the annual increase in hourly wages was about 10 percent; in 1984, it was under 4 percent.

So the *Wirtschaftswunder* was wrought. Yet, as one asks in the television soap operas: Can we have five more uninterrupted years of sustained growth? Will economic expansion pay for or reduce the deficits? Can the administration or the Congress make further spending cuts? Will we have to increase taxes? Will foreign capital continue to flow into the United States, or will the tide begin to run out?

As in politics, so in economic discourse do we find a number of role reversals. In 1980, the Keynesians were downgrading the question of deficits. In the Borg-Warner lectures at the Cornell Business School, in the spring of that year, Robert M. Solow, one of the most-respected and lucid economists of his generation, argued, simply, that the *size* of the deficit was less important than the proportion of deficits to the budget, and to the GNP. Where there was underutilization of capacity, and an "ineffective" demand, deficits were healthy, stimulative, and probably noninflationary. If a small increase in inflation did result, the cost was worth it with respect to the additional employment it generated, the increases in GNP, and even the possible increases in tax revenues from employment. Four years later, Walter Heller and, cautiously, Robert Solow maintained that deficits do matter—at the point where investment becomes crowded out and the inflationary clock is reset.

On the opposite side of the fence, Irving Kristol, the most respected publicist defending the policies of the Reagan administration, reversed his stand in 1980. In 1980, the issue was that deficits are a matter of concern; in 1984, the attitude was that deficits do not matter—much. In 1980, it was believed that monetary policy would provide the necessary restraint on spending; in 1984, the belief was that interest rates mattered more and that tax policy—cutting the marginal rates to stimulate investment—was the decisive policy instrument. In 1980, the belief was that the market, rather than government, knows best, and its judgments should be heeded; in 1984, the belief was that the market is often skittish, short-sighted, and unwilling to rely on faith in the future that Mr. Reagan holds out as promise.

Whatever the starting point of the different evaluations, the crucial figure, as all analysts would perhaps agree, is not the *nominal* budget deficit—that is, the specific monetary shortfall from revenues at any time of the year—but the *structural* budget deficit. The structural budget deficit includes both the cyclically adjusted figure and, more important, the deficit that might remain if (or when) the economy reached a high level of employment, or when the economy reached the level of "potential" GNP (that is, the level of output that it was capable of reaching in the fuller utilization of capacity). In short, it would be the deficit that would remain, even as the economy improved.[8]

The one benchmark would be the reaching of an "acceptable" rate of unemployment consistent with stable prices or an "acceptable" inflation. The other benchmark would be the noninflationary level of *output,* or one that would not start a new inflationary spiral. It is, in short, the kind of economy everyone might like to see: almost everyone employed who wants a job, without pushing up the cost of labor; and the utilization of plant capacity without overheating the economy.

In the colorful grayness of the official language, what once was called the "high employment" measure is now "the standardized-employment" measure. Over time, of course, the level of what is "standard" (of "acceptable" levels of unemployment consistent with "acceptable" levels of inflation) has been successively redefined. Given the startling changes in the labor force, the growth of parttime employment, and the argument as to what would be the "natural rate" of unemployment, many economists differ as to what the "employment benchmark" should be. The Humphrey-Hawkins Bill, enacted as the Full Employment and Balanced Growth Act of 1978, called for an unemployment rate of 4 percent by 1984. Liberal-minded economists now would accept 5 percent as the appropriate rate. More-conservative economists lean to 6 percent.

The idea of the *structural* budget deficit is the fulcrum of economic estimates and policy choices. If a large deficit remained which could not be reduced substantially by economic growth, then the constraints on policy would be all the greater: to raise taxes, cut spending, or increase borrowing (and going deeper into debt) and also risk the crowding out of private investment. The idea of a structural budget deficit was the cause within the administration of the bitter dispute between Martin

Feldstein (supported by David Stockman) in his projection of a high structural budget deficit in the next Reagan years (and therefore the need for new taxes, or at least for a standby tax scheme) and Secretary of the Treasury Donald Regan (supported by Paul Craig Roberts), who denied that there was a relation between high deficits and high interest rates, and who claimed that economic expansion (based upon the stimulative role of investment) would reduce the deficit to manageable proportions in the future.

Yet even here the issues are not clear cut, for the definitions of debt are somewhat ambiguous. What does a federal deficit consist of? The difficulty is that the federal accounting system, unlike that of a business corporation, does not sort out capital assets from immediate spending outlays. Based on nominal numbers, it may not measure the "real market values" of debts, and thus perpetuates a "money illusion." As Robert Eisner, a liberal economist who has made some detailed calculations of the debt and budget figures, remarks:

The high-employment budget currently calculated for an unemployment level of 5.1 percent . . . is fundamentally flawed [and] is not an unbiased measure of fiscal thrust. It in fact measures nominal rather than real impacts on income, and confuses nominal flow with changes in real stocks." As he later wrote, in a more polemical vein: "If the government had used the same accounting practices that private companies use, its 1980 budget deficit of $61 billion would have been cut by a third and the 1981 deficit of $62 billion by $27 billion. The corrections for 1982 and 1983 would have been even larger— $43 billion and $31 billion. But the official deficits then were also much larger—$112 billion and $186 billion.[9]

Paul Craig Roberts, the former Assistant Secretary of the Treasury in the Reagan Administration, has argued that Budget Director David Stockman had been consistently overestimating the budget deficit (one of $231 billion for the fiscal year ending in October, 1984, as against the $175 billion which was the final figure), that the strong economic recovery and the large state and local budget surpluses had reduced the government presence in the credit markets. He concluded that "The projections now show a balanced budget in 1989 instead of a $300 billion deficit." [10]

Mr. Regan (and Mr. Reagan) have argued that there is no direct tie between the large deficit and high interest rates. The proof was provided in the fact that the prime rate fell from 21.5 percent to 11 percent, while the deficit was doubling. It is only the fear of a market that would not confront reality, which demands a discounted premium on expected inflation, that has kept interest rates high. And Regan pins his faith on continued economic expansion and the hope of future reductions in federal expenditures, to reduce the deficit.

While most economists would grant Robert Eisner's point that the federal accounting system hides many assets (which could even be sold off in a pinch, to pay for the deficit and debts!), the theoretical argument does not affect the *recent* situation, since the rising deficit has resulted almost entirely from increased federal spending on defense, social security (broadly defined), and interest on the debt. None of that would be included in a capital budget.

As Robert Heilbroner, in a judicious review of the issues in an essay in *The New Yorker,* remarked that a budget naturally moves towards a balanced condition as employment and output rise. "The alarming aspect of the current budget situation is that this normal relationship has come apart. The huge Reagan tax cuts have reduced federal claims against income by a third . . . in the hope that their buoyant effect on private spending would remain unchanged or even rise. When this hope of 'supply-side economics' failed to materialize, we were left with a tax structure that reduced the inflow of funds to the government. . . ."[11]

The heart of the Reagan strategy has been substantial reductions in the level of taxes and even stronger reductions in the marginal tax rates as a means of stimulating savings and investment. The savings issue is important because, as Charles F. Wolf, Jr., points out, if private savings were higher, deficits would be less troublesome and interest rates would be lower. Yet the puzzling fact is the continuing decline in the personal savings rate even through the Reagan tax-cut years. In 1973, personal savings as a percentage of disposable personal income were 8.6 percent; over the years they have moved downwards, from 6.9 percent in 1981 to 4.8 percent in 1983. The ten-year decline in the U.S. savings rate is all the more extraordinary since it occurred during a period when real personal disposable income rose 15 percent and when, in more recent years, expanded incentives to invest in tax-deferred retirement accounts and more liberal pension-payment deferrals presumably would have stimulated more personal savings. But they have not. Has the fear of inflation become embedded in the "permanent consumption" hypothesis?

Corporate profits have been running high, as a result of substantial tax breaks. *Fortune* has estimated that "the stream of tax-sheltered profits generated by liberal depreciation allowances is running at a rate of more than $50 billion a year." Given corporate tax rates of about 36 percent, this means that corporate borrowing has increased by a like amount. As William C. Freund, the chief economist of the New York Stock Exchange, has remarked: "Never in history has so much of the U.S. economy depended on borrowed money." [12]

However, at the same time that there have been large tax breaks for business, there has been a strong investment binge. *The Economist* (September 1, 1984) estimates that investment by companies accounted for 25 percent of the growth in GNP in the first 18 months of the recovery, while, in previous recoveries, business investment contributed an average of 11 percent of GNP growth in such a period. And yet there remains the large gap between revenues and spending, which is about 19 percent of GNP. And the recurring question remains as to how that will be bridged.

Three more benchmarks have to be added to our picture. One is the federal debt and the interest costs. The debt passed the $1 trillion mark shortly after Mr. Reagan took office. When he leaves office, in 1989, it is likely that it will reach almost $2.5 trillion in fiscal 1989, according to the Congressional Budget Office's latest baseline projections. As a percentage of the gross national product, the debt held by the public would climb from its current level of 35 percent to 46 percent by the end of the decade—assuming, of course, that current government policies are unchanged.

Because of the growth of the debt and high nominal interest rates, net interest costs are currently the fastest-growing part of the federal budget. During the 1960s and 1970s, net interest represented about 7 percent of total budget outlays and less than 2 percent of GNP. In fiscal 1983, net interest outlays totalled $90 billion, or 11 percent of budget outlays. By fiscal 1989, they are projected to be about $214 billion, or 16 percent of total outlays. As a share of GNP, interest outlays would grow from about 3 percent at present, to 4 percent by 1989. [13]

The second benchmark is the extraordinary foreign-trade deficit which the strong dollar has brought about in its pressure against exports. As Arthur F. Burns has pointed out, "It is well to keep in mind that prior to last year, the biggest current account deficit that any country had ever experienced in a single year was about $15 billion. The $70 to $80 billion shortfall that the United States is headed for this year is awesomely different from anything experienced in the past." [14]

But even Burns' mind-boggling statements pale against the reality. The Goldman Sachs Economic Research Report for October 1984 stated that in January it had projected a $120 billion merchandise trade deficit for 1984, about 20 percent larger than most estimates of the time. However, rather than falling, as almost everyone expected, the dollar rose 10 percent on a trade-weighted basis, so that by the first half of 1984, the merchandise trade deficit averaged $120 billion at an annual rate, and in July and August was at a $144 billion annual rate. For a while, the foreign-trade deficit benefited the U.S. economy as a whole (even though some U.S. export-dependent industries suffered), for foreigners used the dollars received for *their* exports to purchase U.S. financial assets, thus helping to finance the federal deficit. *"However, the trade deficit may be reaching levels that are exerting a greater drag on the economy than will be offset by fiscal stimulus. Consequently, in increasing the net export deficit in 1984, we also reduced GNP by a comparable amount."* [15]

The third benchmark is the extent to which the federal deficit, *so far,* has been financed by foreign-capital inflows, which have superceded U.S. savings, and which have crowded out European government borrowing in markets. "We are borrowing abroad at the rate of $80

billion to $90 billion a year,'' Paul Volcker said in his
testimony before Congress on July 25, 1984. But this
heavy borrowing clashes with the borrowing needs of
European nations seeking to finance their own balance-
of-payments deficits. (Sweden, for instance, borrowed
nearly $9 billion in the first half of 1984 simply to refi-
nance existing debt.) All of this creates a competitive
bidding rate. The Thatcher government increased British bank rates 2¾ percent in just two working days this
summer while the German Bundesbank spent $320 mil-
lion, or about 2 percent of its convertible currency, in a
fruitless effort to stem the mark's decline against the dollar
in July. The strong dollar increases the interest cost on
the debt owed by the third-world countries to American
banks. And the fact that the prices of key commodities,
such as oil, are denominated in dollars means that the
strong dollar—between 1980 and mid-1984 it appreciated about 50 percent against the English pound and the
German mark, and 100 percent against the French franc—
increases the cost of such commodities to these countries, as they have to pay more for the dollars they need
to pay for them.

The troublesome question, closer to home, is whether
such support may not suddenly shift and cause a collapse. A fall in the dollar may reverse the tide, and the
capital which has flowed in so quickly (more than doubling in amount in one year's time) may flow out as
readily. That dependency poses a double difficulty. Most
forecasts suggest that we will have to borrow abroad about
2 percent or more of our GNP this year to meet the projected financial needs. As Volcker has remarked: ''That
pace does not seem sustainable over a long period.'' If
we are faced at some point with a reduction in the net
flow of capital from abroad, the burden of financing the

budget deficit would then be thrown back more fully on domestic sources of savings. And then we would be in a bind, since those savings have not increased. If, however, we do continue to seek the flow of funds into our capital and money markets, the dollar will be pushed higher in the exchange markets, we increase our trade and current-accounts deficit, and continue to undercut our worldwide trading position. We cannot have it both ways: to look for foreign funds to finance the deficit and then expect to narrow the widening gap in our trade accounts. "At the end of the day," as Volcker has put it, "the counterpart of a net capital inflow is a net deficit on our current account—trade and services—with other countries. . . . If all the data reflect reality, the largest and richest economy in the world is on the verge of becoming a net debtor internationally, and will soon be the largest." [16]

To return to the baselines. The revised budget-deficit projections put forth by the Congressional Budget Office (taking into account the Deficit Reduction Act of 1984) show deficits of $178 billion in 1985 and $263 billion in 1989, the latter figure just under 5 percent of GNP. (In 1989, outlays would be $1.305 trillion and revenues $1.042 trillion; budget outlays 24.3 percent of GNP, and revenues 19.4 percent, or a budget deficit of 4.9 percent.) As the report concludes:

Despite the deficit-reducing measures enacted since February, CBO expects the structural component of the deficit to continue rising if further budgetary action is not taken. . . . Assuming that no further fiscal policy action is taken, the structural deficit would continue to rise during a projected period of sustained economic growth. This portends a long period of high real interest rates and a consequent evolution in the composition of output toward relatively more consumption and less investment.[17]

Surely not a healthy picture. Surely *some* further budgetary action will have to be taken. But what?

III. Gridlock

Beware the Jabberwock, my son!
The jaws that bite, the claws
*   that clutch!*
Beware the Jubjub bird and shun
The frumious Bandersnatch!

In his *Poetics,* Aristotle writes that "a likely impossibility is always preferable to an unconvincing possibility." The reason, he points out, derives from Homer's use of paralogism, or false conclusions, in his poetry. And conversely, "just because we know the truth of the consequent, we are in our minds led on to the erroneous inference of the truth of the antecedent."

If I apply this reasoning in the present instance, the simple conclusion is that, given the nature of the structural deficit, neither spending cuts nor economic growth will be able to eliminate it and that some sizable tax increase will have to be levied. The only question is whether it will be levied in time. But then, as Aristotle points out in making the distinction between the historian and the poet, it is not that the one writes prose and the other verse, but that the poet deals with "what is possible, as being probable or necessary."[18]

To continue we have to move from rhetoric to prose, and from prose to prosaic statistics. The striking thing

Fiscal Year	Social Programs	Defense Budget
1975	54.5	26.7
1980	55.9	23.2
1983 (est.)	54.3	26.4

SOURCE: *Economic Report of the President,* 1984.

is that over the past ten years, the proportion between social and military spending, as a percentage of total federal spending, has remained roughly the same.

The change has come principally in the "mix" within the two. On the social side, if one looks at the disposable income of the "statically average family" for the period of 1979 to 1984, government benefits went up by 37 percent. But this hid some extraordinary changes within that component.

Actually, the reductions were even smaller than what Mr. Reagan had originally proposed. The president asked for a reduction of 51.7 percent in food stamps, but the actual budgetary outlay was minus 13.8 percent. In welfare, the administration proposed a 28.6 percent reduction, but the final cut was 14.3 percent. In child nutrition, the proposal was minus 46 percent, the actual figure was minus 28 percent. In part, some of the cuts were refused by the Congress; in other measures, the rise in needs created by the recession increased the claimants for welfare, for food stamps, etc., despite the more-

Government Benefits	1971	1979–1984 Change	
Social Security	861	+585	+68 percent
Means-tested cash benefits			
(e.g. welfare)	333	−76	−23 percent
Food stamps	139	−16	−12 percent
Totals:	1,333	+493	+37 percent

SOURCE: Isabel Sawhill and John Palmer, *The Reagan Record* (Washington, D.C.: The Urban Institute, 1984), Chapter 10.

stringent eligibility requirements. In the case of social security, however, the increase was due to the growing number of the elderly, the higher wage base of the new recipients, and the indexing of pensions for cost-of-living allowances. In the case of defense (which we will consider later), the major change was a rise in the weapons component over the previous years.[19]

As the OECD survey reported, "It now seems politically unlikely that very sizeable new cuts will be made in defense, pensions, health and interest expenditures, yet these account for more than 80 percent of total spending. In other areas, the reductions . . . in real ex-

Projected Budget Outlays by Major Category, 1984 and 1987
(in billions of dollars)

	1984	1987	Percent Change 1984 to 1987
National defense[a]	235	331	41.1
Entitlements and other mandatory spending			
Medicaid	21	27	31.9
Other means-tested benefits	40	45	10.6
Social Security	173	211	21.5
Medicare	64	94	45.3
Other nonmeans-tested programs	101	114	12.7
Nondefense discretionary spending	156	178	13.8
Net interest	108	168	55.2
Gross outlays	899	1,167	29.8
Offsetting receipts	−46	−55	18.6
Budget outlays	853	1,112	30.4
Reference: GNP	3,563	4,612	29.4

[a] Assumes 5 percent real growth in the defense-budget authority.

SOURCE: "Reducing the Deficit: Spending and Revenue Options," *Yearly Report of the Congressional Budget Office* (Washington, D.C.: Congressional Budget Office, February, 1984).

penditures on education, training employment and social services were close to 25 percent between 1981 and 1983. . . . Nor does there seem to be much additional scope for reductions in transfers to state and local governments. . . ."[20] Nor can the so-called means-tested entitlement programs, such as food stamps and Aid to Families with Dependent Children be cut further. As John Weicher, of the American Enterprise Institute, stated, "They've gone about as far as they are going to go on low-income benefits programs."[21]

If one returns to the major categories, we see the following constraints.

Defense: The administration is proposing for 1985 to 1987 about 6.5 percent *increases* above the Congressional Budget Office (CBO) baselines.

Social Security: The president has pledged that no further cuts will be made in social security since the revisions in 1983. That puts nearly 20 percent of the gross outlays off limits in any deficit-reduction plan.

Medicare: This is second only to interest payments in the rapidity of growth between 1984 and 1987. If cutting Medicare is to be a major means to reducing the budget deficit, it means either higher health costs for the elderly; lower payments to health-care providers (hospitals and doctors) or diminished use of health services; or a shift of these higher costs to the state and local governments and a consequent increase in local taxes to pay for these reductions.

Infrastructure: Federal highway spending is a growing program, and in 1987 will account for 8.2 percent of all nondefense discretionary outlays. Yet, cutting back on these projects means a reversal of the Surface Transportation Act of 1982, which has been financed by a tax of 5 cents a gallon on gasoline, and thus a repudiation

of a pledge to highway users. What can be more readily
postponed—as it has been already for more than a decade—is work on the declining infrastructure of the society.[22]

Interest Payments: The publicly held federal debt is
projected to increase from 1.3 trillion in 1984 to $2.5
trillion in 1989, or from 35.4 percent of GNP in 1984
to 46 percent in 1989 according to the *revised* budget
outlook update in August 1984. (The earlier one, in
February, had assumed 37.3 and 49 percent, respec-
tively.) The proportion of interest payments to budget
outlays is now projected to rise from 13.1 percent in 1984
to 16.4 percent in 1989. In the 1970s, interest on the
debt averaged about 7 percent of GNP. Now it has almost doubled. If the deficit is not reduced, it will mean
that about 15 or more cents of each taxpayer's dollar will
be used to pay interest, rather than to purchase public
services (such as roads, bridges, water systems, air-
ports, water supply, waste removal, and the like).

Federal borrowing to bridge the deficit gap in 1983
was 6.4 percent of GNP. To reduce the deficit target to
3 percent of GNP in three years, by spending reductions
alone, would mean an across-the-board cut of 10 percent in all, *noninterest,* government spending. Since many
programs are backed by law, or presidential promise (such
as social security), or are inviolable, such as defense,
many programs (including farm support, Medicare and
Medicaid, education, child care, and, most of all, public infrastructure) would inevitably bear the brunt of those
further cuts.

To reach the same 3 percent target on the tax side
would mean an overall federal tax burden of 21 percent
on incomes, which would be just slightly higher than the
20.9 percent of GNP in 1981, the peak level of taxes in

U.S. peace-time history. It would mean, in effect, rescinding all the tax cuts of 1981 and 1982 enacted by the Reagan administration.

Mr. Donald Regan has assumed that if increases in budget outlays can be held to 5 percent a year, beginning in fiscal 1985 (which means zero growth, if inflation is 5 percent) and with the economy growing steadily at 4 percent, then by 1989 the deficit would be close to zero. But Mr. David Stockman takes a less optimistic view. In estimates published by the Office of Management and Budget in August (assuming that all the Administration proposals to cut the budget are enacted), outlays would still increase 9.5 percent for fiscal year 1985, and even if the increase in nominal outlays were held to 5 percent, expenditures would still have to be cut by $124 billion in fiscal 1989. No administration spokesman has indicated where such cuts could be made.

In contrast, some supply-side economists argue that the economy could—will—have a 5.5-percent *real* economic growth from 1985 to 1989, if we climb their faith ladder. The CBO baseline assumes seven years of uninterrupted economic growth, at 4 percent a year, from 1982 to 1989. If one takes the 5.5 percent figure, the deficit would be decreased to $21 billion in fiscal 1989. Yet that prediction is quite shaky indeed. It assumes, for example, that unemployment would fall to 2 percent in 1989—which is four percentage points below the standard mark taken by the Administration economists as consistent with a stable inflation rate. These supply siders, however, have a roseate view of America. Once incentives are released, by entreprenurial activity and soaring productivity, we will make the prosaic business cycle a stodgy remnant of the past. As in *Peter Pan*, we need only believe.

IV. Intermezzo: From Economics to Politics

You see, it is like a portmanteau—there are
two meanings packed into one word.

George Stigler, with the habitual arrogance of every
guildsman expressing the arcane knowledge of his own
specialty, once said that there was more agreement within
the economics profession as a whole than between the
economics profession and the lay public. What is most
evident today is the disarray within the discipline and a
further loss of confidence on the part of the public, let
alone the policymakers (unless they are economists
themselves), in economics.

Almost 50 years ago, in the wake of what is com-
monly called ''The Keynesian Revolution,'' the belief
had arisen that sufficient knowledge had been achieved
for the government to manage the macro economy and
even, in that lovely phrase borrowed from musicians, to
fine tune the instruments. The victory seemed so complete that a dozen or so years ago Mr. Richard Nixon
was reported to have said: ''We are all Keynesians now.''

I first encountered the idea of the positive role of budget deficits in 1942, when, as managing editor of *The
New Leader,* I published a series of essays by Abba P.
Lerner, a young Englishman who was one of the earliest
exponents of Keynes. The title of the series was ''Func-
tional Finance.'' The idea was, simply, that if an economy was stagnant, the government could prime the pump
by spending and incurring debt: an economy was like a
''hydraulic system,'' and one had to get the stagnant
savings circulating down one pipe to get consumption
moving up the other.

There were two corollaries to Lerner's theorem. First,

no government could ever go bankrupt, for, unlike a private individual or firm, all debt was simply "owed to itself," and the government could, if necessary, always recoup the debt by increased taxation. Second, the size of the deficit itself was unimportant; the only relevant consideration was its proportion to GNP. As with a public utility, a budget deficit was simply the cost of borrowing. Most utilities financed their operations largely by debt. None ever "retired" the debt, they simply rolled it over when the bonds came due. Similarly for the economy—with the added advantage that a deficit was stimulative and, if the priming was sufficient, the upturn in economic activities would generate revenues and thus pay off the deficit.

The difficulty with Lerner's ideas, as we have seen in the past 20 years, is that when there is too much priming or borrowing, we create inflation. As Adam Smith observed a long time ago, nations often deal with inflation by "debasing" the coinage to reduce their obligations.[23] Also, sophisticated individuals can create large tax shelters to avoid the higher tax levies. Finally, the national debt may be held by others (particularly other nations) who can refuse to repay their obligations.

The second, more-important Keynesian innovation was the emphasis on what was called "the real economy"— the level of output, the number of jobs, the degree of investment—with less attention to the "nominal" relations expressed in prices and the demand for money. The bridge between the two was "discovered" in 1960 by Paul Samuelson and Robert M. Solow in what is called "the Phillips curve." This was a reformulation by these two M.I.T. economists of the rate of inflation and the level of unemployment in the U.S. "This shows," they wrote, "the menu of choice between different levels of unemployment and price stability as roughly estimated from the last twenty-five years of American data.'' Franco Modigliani, in his Presidential address to the American Economic Association in 1976, argued that ''the stabilization authorities [now] had the power of choosing the unemployment rate around which unemployment was to be stabilized, though it then had to accept the associated inflation.'' [24]

The ''trade off'' was based on the assumption of ''full employment'' of about 3 percent. The difficulty began after the mid-1960s, when the relationship of prices to unemployment became unhinged, and unemployment went on rising along with the rising rates of inflation. In the jargon of the economists, the problem was not the trade off up and down the slope, but the shift of the entire slope to the right. That is, because of a change in the makeup of the labor force (more teenagers, more women moving in and out of the labor force), the rate to which joblessness could be reduced, without touching off more inflation, had now moved to about 6 percent, if not higher. And for many years inflation itself seemed to take on an autonomous life of its own, moving quite independently of the unemployment rate. Neither cost-push nor demand-pull arguments could explain this. So the Phillips Curve seemed to have become largely irrelevant, and the fine tuning had gone sour. [25]

Then, Milton Friedman claimed that unemployment was to be explained as the deviation from its ''natural rate,'' the point where markets would clear if wages were left to fall naturally to the level where employers would hire. Inflation was solely determined by the growth of the money supply. In fact, Friedman wrote, in a remarkable claim, ''. . . there is perhaps no other empirical relation in economics that has been observed to recur so uniformly under so wide a variety of circumstances as the relation between substantial changes over short periods in the stock of money and in prices. . . . This uniformity is, I suspect, of the same order as many of the uniformities that form the basis of the physical sciences."[26]

The question, of course, is, what is money? Friedman has argued that it is pointless to try to define money theoretically or by any set of specific measures. Money, he argues, is whatever category of assets provides the best results in econometric tests of the demand for money. The difficulty with that argument is that much of this may have been true when money was largely a commodity, so that demand might be relatively unambiguous. But with the extraordinary changes we have seen in the nature of financial instruments, and with the extraordinary volatility and velocity of financial transfers, we have many different ways that individuals can monetarize assets and use these for the purposes of money. As Roger Bootle has put it, there is an enormous difference between *commodity* and *credit* money, and "credit money proper may possess none of the key characteristics associated with commodity money."[27]

Recent financial history bears out the fact that new, different credit instruments (such as "repos") are introduced, and, in the extreme situation, as in Israel recently, bank shares begin to substitute for money as the medium of exchange. With the globalization of the capital markets and floating exchange rates, dollars and other currencies can be shifted across borders and wreak havoc with national financial policies.

In the U.S. itself, the orthodox monetarists predicted that an increase in the money supply is followed *by an acceleration of prices within 18 to 24 months*. Thus they

had argued that with the surge of 12 percent in the M-1
measure—currency, demand deposits, and other check-
able accounts—during the second half of 1982 and the
first half of 1983, the inflation rate would be 8 or 9 or
10 percent by the end of 1984. They now find themselves confronting a rate that is half their predictions.
So where is that "uniformity of the physical sciences"?

This is not intended as an excursus into theoretical
economics; it is to make a simpler yet more fundamental point: *Science is only possible where there are reg-
ularities or stable relations, so that we have some as-
surances that the relations we specify between relevant
variables hold over time.* In the physical world, such
variables, difficult as they may be sometimes to discern
or measure, have an intrinsic order. In the social world,
that order is "socially constructed" and subject to change.

The efforts to build a science in the social sphere rests
upon a number of different assumptions. One of the old-
est is that of a "constant" human nature (the desire for
power, for gain, among others). These assumptions may
be true as generalities, but they offer few guides to specific situations. The ideal we find in "neoclassical economics" is the idea of an autonomous, self-contained,
closed system, built upon certain assumptions such as
rationality, maximization, relative prices, and the clear-
ing of markets under conditions of theoretical equilibrium. This is a very powerful "analytical engine." In a
world of stable relations, the constraints of which are
clear, such a model *can* serve as a guide to action. But
that is not often the case. Failing that, the value of the
model may only be "as if," a rational fiction as to what
optional exchange and behavior might be under ideal
conditions, and therefore a standard against which to
understand empirical behavior.

The most-important fact about the last two decades is that these stable economic relations have become unhinged. Market economies use prices as signals as to what, and how much, should be produced and exchanged. But when the price mechanisms become blurred, individuals often do not know how to respond. There are the exogenous shocks from energy prices, to the "dirty floats" of exchange rates which distort efforts to even out balance-of-payments surpluses and deficits. There are political deceptions from Lyndon Johnson's lying about the intended escalation of the U.S. involvement in Vietnam, with its consequent distortion of the budget estimates and the ensuing inflation, to David Stockman's weaseling to the Senate Budget Committee in April, 1981, when he stated that there would be a balanced budget in 1984, rather than a $60 billion deficit projected by the Congressional Budget Office, because the "magic asterisk" in his statement (budget reductions to be announced later by the President) would solve the problem.[28] And all of these are exacerbated because we no longer live in "closed systems," and find ourselves subject more and more to uncertainties from the rapid introduction of new technologies and the multiple political shocks and crises generated by political regimes.

What counts most, as John Maynard Keynes pointed out most cogently, is the nature of *expectations* and our inherent difficulties in plotting these.[29] Traditionally, most economists assume that individuals base their expectations on the past as a means of judging the future. Most econometric models are based on past behavior and assume certain lag effects. The new school or rational expectations, however, assumes that individuals have on hand the information they need and quickly adjust their actions, so that the past is less often a useful guide to the more-or-less instantaneous adjustments (such as a "random walk" in stock prices) which individuals make to present situations. Whatever attitude one takes to these technical questions of modelling, one thing is clear. Many of the old prescriptions are useless because they were based on assumptions of "economically rational" responses to policies. Who would have expected, ten years ago, that it would take a rise of the prime rate to over 20 percent for credit demand to begin to dampen. People simply did not believe that the government would ratchet up the prime rate and thus kept on borrowing. The question is one of credibility and trust. If I can reformulate "rational expectations" in my own terms; *When the political discount rate is higher than the economic discount rate, all rules about calculability dissolve.* That is the bridge to the next sections.

V. "Politics Is Not an Exact Science" (Bismarck, 1863)

Everything's got a moral, if you can only find it.

Ronald Reagan restored the trust of the American people in their society.[30] He did so, in part, because of his unabashed invocation of patriotism, which assuaged the guilt many persons had felt about America's role in the Vietnam War. He did so, in part, by telling the people that they should put less trust in government to solve their problems and that private spending should be used as an indication of what major decisions should be made as to where the economy should go. And he did so, for the most part, because of the economic recovery and the sense the American people had that with Mr. Reagan it would continue.

Yet, it is also clear that much of Mr. Reagan's success was strongly correlated with the performance of the economy. As the recession took hold in the fall of 1981, and unemployment rose, more and more persons reported being worse off than before, and the president's popularity plummeted accordingly. Gallup found 48 percent of persons saying they were better off in May 1981, and 37 percent reporting being worse off; by March 1983, the figures were almost exactly reversed. From a high of 69 percent of popularity in April and May 1981, support dropped to 40 percent between January and March 1983, according to Roper. Yet, in November 1984, as Democratic pollster Dotty Lynch reported after the election, 58 percent of the voters felt they were better off than four years ago, and of these 87 percent voted for Ronald Reagan.[31]

It would be wrong to say that this was a "personal" victory for Mr. Reagan. But neither was it a "Republican" victory. The number of Republican House seats gained was considerably lower than it had been four years before; it did not recoup the loss of seats in 1982. The change in the Senate was a shade in the favor of the Democrats. Mr. Reagan ran as a "national" figure, appealing to the economic record, and traditional values, and not as a party figure. In fact, the "radical right" was so furious with the campaign that on the Monday after the election, Richard Vigurie wrote an article for the op-ed page of the *New York Times* under the headline, "Reagan's Campaign Double-Crossed the G.O.P."[32]

Much of the difficulty in understanding the crosscurrents of American politics, I would argue, is that most commentators (and many academics) have been predicting and awaiting a "realignment" in the American parties. The argument (from Walter Dean Burnham to Kevin Phillips) has been that just as there was a "fundamental" realignment of political forces in 1983, so there would be one of "an emergent Republican majority"—except that such an emergence was deflected by Mr. Nixon's Watergate debacle in 1972.

In 1932, Franklin Delano Roosevelt did gain new support from the nascent trade-union movement, the party change of the Midwestern farmers (and "progressive Republicans"), and the urban Northern machines, while keeping the traditional Democratic South. The assumption was that the Republicans would also create a new alignment. But of whom? The difficulty is that these analyses misread the greater complexity of American society today—the demographic, technological, and geographical changes—and the increasing difficulty in isolating consistent clusters of voters, other than a few sharply focussed groups, such as the blacks. If I look at American society today, I would identify these modal changes as affecting the nature of the polity.

First, there has been a shrinkage of the trade-union movement in the country and the number of industrial workers. Factory workers today account for only 17 percent of the labor force. Other than some government workers (including teachers), the trade-union movement has been unable, for almost 25 years, to stop the erosion of its strength, which is a reflection of the erosion of industrial society.

There have been demographic changes. Fully one-third of the population today is concentrated within an 18-year age span, extending from the late teens to the midthirties. This is a generation whose only scarifying experience has been the Vietnam war, but which, by and large, has lived within the scope of an expanding economy and of the increased levels (leaving quality aside) of education. These younger voters describe themselves consistently in the polls as "antiparty people," deliberately splitting their tickets in an expression of personal autonomy and a rebuke to the organized power brokers and groups.[33]

Geographical shifts in population have taken place from the industrial North Central States, to the Pacific coast, the Rocky Mountains, and Southwest regions, in part because of the search for new energy sources, and, more, the location of "high-tech" and aerospace industries. What we see here is a phenomenon of a large number of new business start-ups through entreprenurial initiative, the reduction of plant and firm size, and a greater dispersal of work and living sites. The traditional Democratic concentrations have been reduced.

We have become, in occupation and income, a middle-class society in fact as well as image. More than 25 percent of the labor force today is professional and technical and managerial, an extraordinary figure for any society. About 48 percent of families have incomes over $25,000 a year. (About 18 percent earn less than $12,500; about 35 percent between $12,500 and $25,000.) More people have a stake in the society.

Political parties have declined in importance to the electorate. Voters no longer see parties as relevant to the conduct of government or their own decisions. They are indifferent to them.[34] Forty-one percent of voters say they are Democrats, 27 percent Republican, and 32 percent Independent. Yet in describing their general point of view, 18 percent say they are liberal, 46 percent moderate, and 30 percent conservative.

As David Broder points out: "There is no precedent in American history for a party so skimpy in its grass-roots strength exercising so near a monopoly on the highest office in the land as the Republicans have done." But it is not as "Republicans" that that party has won the presidency so often since 1952.

There is, in effect (as there has been for some time), a dual structure: the *presidency,* where the symbolic and confidence issues of leadership or character predominate; and the *Congress,* where "interests" and local issues count most. And there is no consistent correlation between the two.

One of the major results of the division between the president and Congress is that the choice of a president focuses on celebrity, personality, character, and "image!"[35] This has long been true and explains why so many U.S. presidents have been successful war generals. But this feature of personality is now enlarged by the television medium. At the same time, the fragmentation of the polity encourages special-interest and single-issue groups in which, increasingly, cultural and symbolic issues (such as religious beliefs about abortion) cut across economic and ethnic and age divisions.

If there is a distinct party realignment, it is in the South. Republicans doubled the number of both their House and Senate seats in North Carolina, and picked up six House seats in both South Carolina and Florida and three in Arkansas. The situation is simply that, as the blacks have worked to increase the registration of voters in the Democratic party, there has been a backlash in which increased white registration has benefitted the Republican party. Reversing a hundred-year history, the South may become Republican again, but it will be a very different kind of Republicanism than that of Abraham Lincoln.

To return, and to emphasize the major social fact, this is now primarily a middle-class society, made up largely of individuals who have only come into the middle class in the past 20 years or so, and who feel strongly about protecting their achievements. In all this, there is a "revolutionary" irony in political philosophy and practice. Historically, the problem of democracy has been rooted, as Aristotle stated, in the fear that if "justice is made to consist of the will of the majority, that majority will be sure to act unjustly . . . and to confiscate the property of the richer minority."[36]

This was the problem that troubled the founders of American society. Their "solution" was to create a republic, a representative government rather than a society based on plebiscite, with checks and balances, and with the Senate elected by the states, rather than directly by the people. The sociological theorem which modified these fears was the idea of equal opportunity and economic growth. If men and women had the chance to rise, and if wealth could be obtained by one's own efforts, then the "zero-sum" game of rich and poor could be avoided.

Today, the basic paradox is that the *haves* outnumber the *have nots*. And it is becoming difficult for any have-not group to "vote themselves" advantages on the basis of electoral strength alone. The turning point was the tax revolts a number of years ago, symbolized by Proposition 13 in California and Proposition 2½ in Massachusetts. In business, the "bottom line" is profit. In politics, it is taxes. The voters have "revolted"—and the significant point is that these restrictions were enacted not by legislatures, but mandated by popular referenda. The fact that in 1984 a number of more-restrictive measures on the taxing powers of the states were voted down does not contradict this basic point.

The crucial question, then, is the economic fate of the middle class. Apart from the elderly—for in the end we are all elderly, and therefore all have a stake in those benefits—can disadvantaged minorities find electoral means of bettering their status? More directly, if the budget deficit is to be reduced, and if it cannot come significantly from reductions in social spending, who will bear the consequent tax burdens? The bulk of the tax benefits from the 1981 and 1982 legislation was received by those with incomes between $20,000 and $80,000. Households in this range received about 70 percent of the total reduction in 1982, a figure which, if unchanged, will rise to approximately 80 percent by 1985.[37]

Yet, if new taxes are to be levied, they can only be levied on that middle class, which has already benefited from tax cuts. That is Mr. Reagan's dilemma. And that is the issue which brings us to our final section.

VI. What Is to Be Done?

"That's the reason they're called lessons,"
the Gryphon remarked, "because they lessen
from day to day."

Ronald Reagan restored a sense of trust in the society. But in the economy? Or has it all been a juggling act? Mr. Reagan has consistently asked for a constitutional amendment to require a balanced federal budget, stating that if we had such an amendment, the deficit would be eliminated. Yet, in his 1981 program, Mr. Reagan increased defense spending, cut back on social spending, cut taxes, and found himself with the largest deficits and the greatest trade imbalances of any president in U.S. history. On January 20, 1985, when Mr. Reagan takes office for the second time, the federal budget will take a larger share of the GNP—from 23.5 percent in fiscal 1981 to 23.9 percent in fiscal 1985— than it did when he took office in 1981.

There is, second, the persistence of the *structural deficit,* which, despite the course of economic growth in the last year or two, in puzzling fashion, has not been reduced. As Benjamin M. Friedman, the Harvard economist who specializes in monetary policy, has observed

Fiscal policy since year-end 1981 has entered uncharted territory in two respects. First, in the wake of the 1981–2 recession, the federal government's expenditures have exceeded its revenues by a margin that was unprecedented in the nation's prior peacetime experience, and not just absolutely but in relation to the size of the economy. Second, *the subsequent return* to economic expansion has not significantly narrowed the budget gap, because the growing fundamental imbalance between federal expenditures and revenues on a full-employment basis has enlarged the deficit about as fast as the return toward full employment has narrowed it.[38]

Finally, as *The Economist* stated on October 27, 1984: "Although Mr. Reagan's ultra-Keynesian America is barrelling along towards full employment, all its trading and budget accounts are frighteningly out of balance. A sound international economic order cannot be built on the assumption that the rumbustiously richest country will go on borrowing unprecedented amounts at enormous interest rates from everybody else forever."

So there is a day of reckoning to come. And its consequences will affect not only the United States but the international economic order as well.

Understandably, the public is concerned. A poll by *Time* at the beginning of the year found that 90 percent of the voters viewed the federal deficit as a serious economic problem. Consistently over the years, between 60 to 70 percent of the population have favored a balanced budget.[39] Yet any sophisticated observer quickly learns to discount such general sentiments. There is a distinction, going back to Jeremy Bentham, between a *social decision* and the *sum total of individual decisions,* as registered either in the economic or political marketplace. A social decision is a symbolic one, giving us a sense of what most people agree to. A government may ask individuals to refrain from purchasing clothes in order to reduce private consumption during wartime. Most people might say yes, but someone fingering his threadbare garment might also say, "I need a suit," and the total of individual decisions will have a different outcome from the social one. This is not to say that a social decision is always a facade, or simply an ideological acquiescence. Under conditions of strong adversity and strong leadership, a symbolic appeal may be a powerful incentive to consensus. In most situations, however, the private interests supersede, and the aggregate consequences often vitiate the social or symbolic affirmations. As S. M. Lipset has pointed out, for example, national polls show Americans are generally in favor of reducing spending and cutting taxes, but the same polls show substantial majorities support the specific programs that constitute the welfare state. When Ronald Reagan took office, the majority of the population favored increases in defense spending even at the expense of social programs. As the recession deepened and unemployment rose, the weight of opinion shifted sharply. It is quite possible that in the last two years, the sentiments have shifted again in the opposite direction. So "public opinion" is not a very sure guide to actual views.

The same problem applies in the political marketplace. The Grace Commission, appointed by President Reagan, "identified $424.4 billion in savings and added revenue that could be realized over three years without affecting necessary social programs and raising taxes." As Mr. Grace observed in an op-ed piece in the *New York Times* (September 27, 1984)

An example of waste: subsidized rates for electric power from Western generating facilities were extended for 30 years at a time when the nation faces the worst fiscal crisis ever. How can Congress justify preferable power rates ranging from 7 to 25 percent of the rates paid by 85 percent of the taxpayers— a subsidy not for the poor or needy, but the lucky.

What Mr. Grace did not say, as George F. Will pointed out, "The vote in the Republican-controlled Senate was 64 to 34, with every Senator from the west of Missouri voting to continue the subsidy. That is Reagan country, pardner. . . ."[40]

It was once thought that a formal rein could be imposed on the budget process to clarify the choices and reconcile the different claims. Ten years ago, the Congress enacted the Congressional Budget and Impoundment Control Act, which was hailed as the basis for an orderly reform and control of the budget process.[41] For the first time, Alice Rivlin states, the Congress had authority to define and shape the broad strategic issues of budgeting and economic policy. The new procedures brought the spending and revenue sides of the budget together, requiring explicit consensus by vote on three issues: the size of federal spending and revenues; the allocation of resources among major functions (such as defense, health, and agriculture); and the size of the federal deficit. Under the new procedures, the Congress could deal with—indeed, was forced to deal with—the larger issues of the shape and magnitude of the federal budget, not just the internal minutiae.

What has happened, in fact, as Mrs. Rivlin points out in a later assessment, is that the Congress becomes preoccupied almost entirely with the "internal minutiae," for that is how one protects one's constituents.[42] Each year Congress is supposed to vote an overall budget resolution providing an overall summation of the appropriations and revenue measures. In 1984 the Republican leadership argued against adopting such a resolution because of the weariness of the process and the contradictory character of the results. Finally, after tedious debate, one was passed. The extraordinary—or perhaps ordinary—fact is that nobody noticed or paid much attention to it.

As David Stockman, himself a former Congressman, observed "There is a breakdown in the Congressional machinery. There are 100 gauntlets and 1,000 vetoes on Capitol Hill. You simply can't sustain any kind of policy through that process, whether it's the conduct of foreign affairs, the shaping of the budget, or the management of the fiscal affairs of the nation, because there are 180 subcommittees with overlapping jurisdictions and huge staffs. All of these actors want to get into the process and as a result, everybody has their hooks on everything."[43]

So, what will be done?

The administration talks of making major cuts. One major area could be the farm-price-support program. Under the 1981 farm bill, which expires in 1985, federal payments to farmers were increased from $4 billion to over $19 billion last year, which almost equalled the total of farm income. Support payments are indexed to cover expected increases in farmers' costs. If payments were kept at their current levels, the freeze would reduce the cost of the agricultural programs to about $12 billion per year by the end of the decade. Yet farm income has suffered most heavily of that of any group in the country, and the influence of the farm bloc in Congress is still high. (Would Jesse Helms countenance any reduction in the loan guarantees to tobacco farmers?)

The designated increases in the current federal budget are not for new programs, but to cover inflation and demographic changes, such as an aging population. So, simply slowing the rate of spending will reduce someone's benefits, of course. But whose? Military retirement pensions have gone from $10.1 billion in 1980 to $15.9 billion in 1983, and are projected to rise to $20.1 billion in 1987. Civil Service retirement has gone from $14.7 billion in 1980 to $20.6 billion in 1983 and is projected to rise to $27.1 billion in 1987. Do these come under the exclusionary rule of Mr. Reagan's regarding the elderly?[44]

One could eliminate the wool and mohair payment program. Under the National Wool Act of 1949, the program "was enacted as a measure of national security and general economic welfare, because shorn wool was considered an essential and strategic commodity." That would provide a cumulative $580 million savings over five years. One could narrow elementary and secondary education aid and save $1.070 billion cumulatively over five years. In short, one could pick up a billion here and a billion there, but as Bunker Hunt was recently reported to say, a billion dollars is not very much these days.[45]

One could hope for a high, sustained, and long-term

economic growth. Supply-side economics focuses on production and investment. Demand management forced us to choose between inflation or higher unemployment; by concentrating on tax cuts and incentives, business will be induced to expand output and provide more jobs. Much of the difficulty with the initial enthusiasm for tax cuts and incentives was the claim put forth by Arthur Laffer and popularized by Jude Wanniski, that a tax cut would so stimulate economic activity that the resulting revenue would pay for the initial tax cut, thus providing a "free lunch" and contradicting Milton Friedman.[46]

Paul Craig Roberts, who had been an Assistant Secretary of the Treasury, states vehemently in his book *The Supply-Side Revolution* and in his columns in *Business Week* (such as one written for the November 12, 1984 issue) that "supply-side economics is not the Laffer curve." Roberts emphasizes the role of taxes (and marginal tax rates in particular) as incentives that induce people to expand productive activities with the expectation of keeping the larger share of the after-tax income. While this theorem may be true for those individuals who have such choices to make, it does not offer much hope to predict the level of output, the character of prices, and the degree of inflation in a modern economy.

That tax policy may be a crucial variable in capital formation, through capital depreciation accounts, is an idea that any economist would accept. And the fiscal stimulation provided, in part, by the government's accelerated "cost-recovery" provisions, and the investment tax credit, did promote investment in the past two years. But two crucial points need to be noted. In many instances, because of the more-favorable treatment of fixed plant equipment, older and heavy industries benefited at the expense of the new "high-tech" fields. More importantly, while $130 billion was spent in 1984 for direct expenditures, loan guarantees, and tax "breaks" for business, the revenue shortfall which resulted, in part, brought about the large and heavy deficit of $175 billion or more that the nation needs to meet this fiscal year, and those projected in the next several years. We grow, but not enough.

And then there are taxes. No one, of course, likes the present tax code. Everyone is for reform. That is the *social* (or symbolic) decision. But how do we sum up the total of individual points of view? That some kind of "tax simplification" will come forth is a distinct possibility, though various Republican leaders are pressing for spending cuts as the first priority.

If one looks at federal revenues by source as a percent of total revenues, an interesting picture emerges, as can be seen in the accompanying table:

Federal Revenues by Source As a Percent of Total Revenues

Year	Individual Income Taxes	Corporation Income Taxes	Social Insurance Taxes	Excise Taxes	Estate and Gift Taxes	Other
1960	44.0	23.2	15.9	12.6	1.7	2.5
1967	41.3	22.8	22.0	9.2	2.0	2.0
1971	46.1	14.3	25.3	8.9	2.0	3.4
1977	44.3	15.4	29.9	4.9	2.1	3.3
1981	47.7	10.2	30.5	6.8	1.1	3.6
1983	48.1	6.2	34.8	5.9	1.0	4.0

SOURCE: *Reducing the Deficit: Spending and Revenue Options* (Washington, D.C.: U.S. Congressional Budget Office, February 1984), Table VI-1, p. 185.

Clearly, corporations have benefited from the tax revisions. The effective rate of the Federal income tax for corporations under the least-progressive set of incident assumptions was 2.6 percent in 1980. By 1985 it is estimated that it will be 1.7 percent. The share of revenue paid by corporations is only 6.3 percent. That share has been reduced sharply by "tax expenditures," an odd euphemism, since it is not an outlay but money *foregone* by the government if taxes had been levied (rather than permitting the oil and fuel depletion allowances, the investment tax credit, the Accelerated Cost Recovery system, and the like). In fiscal 1986, the direct expenditures to business by the government will come to $23.3 billion. The "tax expenditures" will be to $62.8 billion. The government will allow $150.5 billion in aid to business.[47] How much of these are justified?

One area of tax redress is to impose excise taxes, which have been decreased from 12.6 to 5.9 percent. Joseph Pechman estimates that $35 billion could be raised in 1989 by extending the excise taxes on cigarettes and gasoline now scheduled to expire, doubling the taxes on alcoholic beverages, which have not been touched since 1951, and enacting a further tax on oil as a means of encouraging conservation. Such arguments six revenue with social purposes (such as reducing gasoline consumption); but then, all proposals do.

For the time being, all speculation on the benefits of tax increases may be beside the point. President Reagan has given his solemn word that he will not increase taxes, either directly or indirectly in the guise of tax reform. And one has to accept his word as a variable in the equation—in both the mathematical and lexical senses of the term.

There is one other influence on the national budget, of course—the Federal Reserve Board, meaning Paul Volcker. As I indicated at the start, what has given the economy its extraordinary stability in recent years was a highly stimulative fiscal policy, initiated by the president, balanced against a restrictive monetary policy by Paul Volcker. In that situation, we have survived and may yet continue to. By emphasizing cuts, by lengthening the playout of appropriations (as is already happening in the defense budget), by making incremental increases in taxes, the fiscal stimulative effects may be reduced. And, conversely, the Fed may loosen its somewhat restrictive policies, and accommodate to the new situation.

In the short run, therefore, in the next two years, the major issue may be managing the "recession" (which itself tends to dampen interest rates), and maintaining the stability of the banking and financial system, if a deeper recession takes hold. Further borrowing may make the deficit itself manageable, particularly if the Fed follows an accommodating policy. Further debt, of course (even if the *rate* of increase is slowed down), does levy a new, constant burden on the government, and the large interest payment has its own redistributive effects. But that is a cost the administration is willing to pay with respect to its own priorities in social policy.

VII. Coda

What I tell you three times, is true.

The subject of this paper has been the "structural deficit" and the difficulties we may encounter in reducing it. There are, however, three other "structural" problems which pose different, more diffuse, yet in the long run stronger challenges to the stability of the society. Necessarily, in a coda, I can only be schematic.

The New International Division of Labor

We are facing a new international division of labor, in which the older division, of a set of core Western manufacturing societies, and a periphery of "third-world" nations, is changing rapidly. Part of this change is due to the extension of capitalism throughout the world, a process foretold many years ago by the apocalyptic voice of a revolutionary prophet. That prophet, of course, was Karl Marx, and this is what he wrote in 1848, in *The Communist Manifesto:*

The bourgeoisie has through its exploitation of the world market given a cosmopolitan character to production and consumption in every country. To the great chagrin of reactionaries, it has drawn from under the feet of industry to national ground on which it stood. All old-established national industries have been destroyed or are daily being destroyed. They are dislodged by new industries, whose introduction becomes a life and death question for all civilized nations, by industries that no longer work up indigenous raw material, but raw material drawn from the remotest zones; industries whose products are consumed, not only at home, but in every quarter of the globe. In place of the old wants, satisfied by the productions of the country, we find new wants, requiring for their satisfaction the products of distant lands and climates. In place of the old local and national seclusion and self-sufficiency, we have intercourse in every direction, universal inter-dependence of nations.

More of the change has been the result of the new technology, with the result that the routinized and labor-intensive industries of the old industrial base can be adopted rapidly in other parts of the world. This is now a global society, tied together by communications. Markets are worldwide, in particular capital markets and commodity markets, in which comparative advantage and profit are no longer commanded by resource advantage and labor costs. The United States, at its center has become increasingly a high-tech and headquarters economy (of financial, technical, and professional services) in which its older manufacturing base has to make a transition to the newer modes of specialized, and high value-added, flexible (and even automated) production. Managing this transition requires some coherent industrial policy. It must be coherent not in the sense of a plan or directives, for that only introduces rigidity, but in an awareness of direction and a realization that the most-potent instrument of industrial policy, namely taxes, may be pointing us in the wrong way. Rhetorically, the administration is oriented to entreprenurial initiative. But Mr. Reagan is superb at rhetoric. At some point, however, words have to give way to action.

The Practice of Concurrent Majorities

All the government textbooks tell us that we are a unique combination of a federal administrative system and an electoral democracy in which majority rules. In a formal sense, this is indeed the case, most importantly in the selection of the president (though technically, of course, an individual with a popular minority may gain an electoral majority). In practice, however, we have long been moving towards, and in the legislative process may have even institutionalized, what John C. Calhoun, in his *Disquisition on Government,* called "the doctrine of concurrent majority." Calhoun, of course, believed in states' rights and thought that we were, in effect, "two nations.'' Therefore, each segment should have the right of nullification—or what we would today call veto power—over major actions of the other. (The Civil War was fought in part to establish the principle of the Union and of national rule.)

Given the formalized nature of interest blocs in the country, the *de facto* reality, in particular in economic policy, is that the interests of each major segment are taken into account, and given their due. It is what the political scientist Arend Lijphart calls ''consociational democracy.''[48] In one sense this is a useful principle to contain potentially divisive conflict, especially if Aristotle's caution is heeded, and if continuing opportunity and economic expansion are visible. Yet there are two other risks as well. One is that a form of ''corporatism,'' in which the major economic blocs make their own accords, as against a national idea, sets in. The other is of multiple fragmentation, which we first saw in the cities, and now has spread to the national polity itself. On issues of defense and foreign policy, given the sharper, adversarial nature of the problem, a national policy is still more possible, despite varied ideological differences within. But since economics today is *political* economy, the problem of ''concurrent majorities,'' or ''multiple concurrent minorities,'' becomes a prescription either for *immobilisme* or for compromises, not national policy.

The Passions and the Interests

Albert Hirschman showed how the pursuit of material interests, so long denounced as avarice, became the approved means to contain the unruly and destructive passions of men. The surging role of passion was long ago recognized as the most powerful force in a society. Plato's *Republic* is devoted to the theme of how the wise philosopher, coming out of his cave, would become the tutor to the ''spirited,'' who would become the guardians of society. The rule of reason over the passions and the appetitive natures of men was the basis of Western philosophy, especially when, as in Thomism, this was joined to the power of religion.

Beginning with Hobbes (and the civil wars of passion) and the great merchant adventurers (and pirates), the acquisitive nature of men became feared as the primary force threatening the old hierarchies of society. The political arguments for capitalism, from Montesquieu and James Steuart through Adam Smith, as Hirschman showed, were that ''the calm desire for wealth'' (the phrase of Francis Hutcheson, the teacher of Adam Smith) would provide a means whereby the pursuit of interest could channel the passions of men into gain for all.[49]

I am not interested, especially in a conclusion, in retracing a complicated paradox in the history of ideas. My cautionary tale is contemporary—that the argument still has force if one substitutes the word ''ideology'' for ''passions.'' When the multiplication of interests that may be inevitable in a complex society become crossed by a polarization of ideologies, in which the politicization of social and cultural issues ignites passions and heat, the results are potentially destructive of the polity.

The point about symbolic or ideological issues is that they are, by their nature, *nonnegotiable,* and force partisans and antagonists into a yes/no, either/or frame of mind. The nature of interests is that they are resolvable through negotiation. (The transmutation of the ''labor issue'' from an ideological into an interest issue is what gave this country stability after deep and violent conflict for seventy years.) Since views of morality and religion are not negotiable, liberal theory from Locke to Kant saw the solution in the relegation of such issues to the private sphere, and the restriction on use of public coercion to impose a private view of morality or religion on the society as a whole.

The breakdown of a distinction between the public and private is a troublesome one for the society. But what also risks trouble today is the subtle ''ideologizing'' of economic issues, and even converting them into ''moral'' ones with all the compulsions that lie behind moral beliefs. That is what some ideologists of capitalism are doing today. When the economic and evangelical issues become fused into a single doctrine, then we are in double trouble. It only leads to the hunting of a snark.

Notes

1. John R. Opel, while chairman of International Business Machines, said during the keynote address at the annual meeting of the American Association for the Advancement of Science, on May 24, 1984

The most immediate [need] is to regain our fiscal sanity. In the past 30 years the United States has had exactly four balanced budgets. Our national debt today exceeds $1.5 trillion—nearly $7000 for every American alive. To pay the interest on that debt costs us today 16 percent of our federal revenues. In addition, we face an unprecedented series of future deficits of $200 to $300 billion a year. If these deficits persist, it will mean higher interest rates, a renewal of recession, a renewal of inflation, or all three.

(*Science,* Vol. 1, 225, [July 27, 1984], pp. 378–379.)

2. In *Business Week,* October 22, 1984, in the ''Commentary'' column, Anthony Bianco opens with a quotation

The connection that's been made again between the deficit and the interest rate—there is no connection between them.

(President Reagan, October 7, 1984.)
Bianco then continues

While debate rages among economists over the relationship between budget deficits and interest rates, down in the trenches of Wall Street, there is no debate at all. Among traders, money managers and investment strategists, a $200 billion deficit matters a lot. . . . The market's skittishly perverse behavior over the past two years almost certainly can be traced to the concern over the deficits. . . . The one constant throughout this bewildering period has been the deficit-phobia. . . .

3. Herbert Stein, *Presidential Economics* (New York: Simon and Schuster, 1984).

4. S. M. Lipset, *The Economy, Elections, and Public Opinion,* Working papers in Political Science No. P-83-1 (Stanford, Calif.: Hoover Institution, Stanford University, 1984).

5. Daniel Bell, "The Future World Disorders," *The Winding Passage* (New York: Basic Books, 1981), p. 225.

6. Of the overall budget of $950 billion in the current fiscal year, the defense spending is $36 billion greater than what it would have been under the projected Carter program. Social programs were $59 billion smaller. In percentage terms, military spending went from 22.6 percent of the budget in 1981 to 26.8 percent in the current fiscal year. Nonmilitary spending went down from 67.5 percent to 59.5 percent in that period.

7. *Occasional Paper No. 30* (Washington, D.C.: International Monetary Fund, July 1984), pp. 10–11.

8. For a detailed, if cumbersome, definition of the structural-budget-deficit concept as used in the government, see "Appendix B. Understanding and Measuring the Structural Federal Deficit," in *The Economic Outlook:* A Report to the Senate and House Committees on the Budget—Part 1 (Washington, D.C.: The Congressional Budget Office, February 1984), pp. 103–118.

9. The technical and detailed arguments and calculations appear in Robert Eisner and Paul J. Pieper, "A New View of the Federal Debt and Budget Deficits," *American Economic Review,* Vol. 74, No. 1 (March 1984). See also a supplementary essay, Robert Eisner,

"Which Budget Deficit? Some Issues of Measurement and Their Implications," *American Economic Review,* Vol. 74, No. 2 (May 1984). The popular statement is the essay "Deficit Madness," an op-ed article in the *New York Times* (July 14, 1984).

10. Paul Craig Roberts, "The Deficit Scare Has All But Faded Away," *Business Week* (June 25, 1984), p. 16; "Hard Evidence That Dispels Myths about the Deficit," *Business Week* (May 21, 1984). "How Stockman Really Cooked the Books," *Business Week* (September 17, 1984).

11. Robert Heilbroner, "Reflections: The Deficit," *The New Yorker* (July 30, 1984), p. 54.

12. Bruce Steinberg, "Why You Can't Love the Deficit," *Fortune* (October 15, 1984), p. 40.

13. *Federal Debt and Interest Costs, Special Study, 1984* (Washington, D.C., Congressional Budget Office).

14. Arthur F. Burns, "The American Trade Deficit in Perspective," *Foreign Affairs* (Summer 1984), p. 1068. The text was adapted from a speech given in April 1984.

15. Goldman Sachs Economic Research, *The Pocket Chartroom* (October 1984). Emphasis in the original.

16. From the annual statement on Federal Reserve policy to the House Committee on Banking, February 7, 1984, reprinted in *Challenge* (March–April, 1984), pp. 6–7.

17. *The Economic and Budget Outlook: An Update,* (Washington, D.C.: Congressional Budget Office, August 1984). (The figures are from Table III-1, p. 55; the quotation from p. 50.)

One can add to this warning that of the OECD examiners, who, in their national survey, reported

There appears to be little cause for concern about prospects for 1984; the recovery is well established and should last comfortably through the year. But some of the short-term worries about the pro-cyclical nature of the [fiscal and monetary] mix suggest that some endogenous tightening of conditions could bring undesired deceleration even by 1985—very early by the standards of past recoveries. . . .

There has been no evidence of any correlation between federal deficit and monetary provision over the last business cycle. *However, it is clear that if real interest rates exceed real GNP growth . . . then interest payments and deficits will cumulate in relation to GNP.* Hence if the present policy mix were pursued indefinitely, *given present estimates of the deficit and the growth of potential output, the pattern of development would become unsustainable.*

. . . The key to improved balance lies with fiscal policy and measures to reduce the structural deficit.

OECD Economic Surveys, *United States,* [December 1983 (Washington, D.C.: PECD)], p. 60. Emphasis added.)

18. Aristotle, *Poetics,* Chapter 24, # 1460a and Chapter 9, # 1451b, *The basic Works of Aristotle,* edited by Richard P. McKeon (New York: Random House, 1941), pp. 1482, 1463–1464.

19. *Reducing the Deficit: Spending and Revenue Options. A Report to the Senate and House Committee on the Budget.* (Washington, D.C.: Congressional Budget Office, February 1984), Part III.

20. OECD Economic Surveys, op. cit., pp. 55–56.

21. *Fortune,* Vol. 110, No. (October 1, 1984), p. 27.

22. For a detailed statement on the incredible deterioration of the public infrastructure of the U.S., see: *Public Works Infrastructure: Policy Considerations for the 1980s* (Washington, D.C.: Congressional Budget Office, 1983). As Senator Daniel P. Moynihan remarked in 1983 in the Robert Weinberg lecture at the New York University Club, in constant dollars public-works spending by all levels of government declined nearly 30% over the last decade. Given his taste for paradox, Senator Moynihan pointed out that ''The United States Army Corps of Engineers is now engaged in more construction in Saudi Arabia than in the United States.''

23. As Smith wrote

When national debts have once been accumulated to a certain degree, there is scarce, I believe, a single instance of their having been fairly and completely paid. . . .
The raising of the denomination of the coin has been the most usual expedient by which a real publick bankruptcy has been disguised under the appearance of a pretended payment . . . A national debt of about a hundred and twenty-eight millions, nearly the capital of the funded and unfunded debt of Great Britain, might in this manner be paid with about sixty-four millions of our present money. . . . A pretended payment of this kind, therefore, instead of alleviating, aggregates in most cases the loss of creditors of the publick; and . . . extends the calamity to a great number of innocent people. It enriches in most cases the idle and profuse debtor at the expense of the industrious and frugal creditor.

(''The Nature and Causes of Public Debts,'' *An Inquiry into the Nature and Causes of the Wealth of Nations,* edited by R. H. Campbell and A. S. Skinner, [Oxford: The Clarendon Press, 1976], Volume 2, pp. 929–930.)

24. I have discussed the development of the Phillips Curve argument in my essay "Models and Reality in Economic Discourse," *The Crisis in Economic Theory,* edited by Daniel Bell and Irving Kristol (New York: Basic Books, 1981), pp. 65–69. The sources of the quotations are given there.

25. The irony is that with the recent decreases in inflation and unemployment, the Phillips Curve now seems to be shifting back to the left, to the relationships of a quarter of a century ago!

26. Milton Friedman, "The Quantity Theory of Money—A Restatement," *Studies in the Quantity Theory of Money* (Chicago: University of Chicago Press, 1965).

27. Roger Bootle, "Origins of the Monetarist Fallacy—The Legacy of Gold," *Lloyd's Bank Review* (July, 1984).

28. William Greider, *The Education of David Stockman,* (New York: E. P. Dutton, 1982), pp. 37–38. Mr. Stockman, incidentally, was responding to the fears generated by Henry Kaufman, who predicted large budget deficits.

29. In an article in the *Quarterly Journal of Economics,* a year after the publication of the *General Theory* (he was replying to criticisms of Taussig, Leontieff, Robertson, and Viner), Keynes stated that there would always be inherent disequilibria in the economic system because of the uncertainty of our knowledge, the inability to know the consequences of our actions, the impossibility of making forecasts and of knowing, therefore, what capital returns or discount rates of capital might be. "About these matters," Keynes wrote, "there is no scientific basis on which to form any calculable probability whatever. We simply do not know." (*Pace,* Milton Friedman.)

30. The rising degree of mistrust has been one of the more alarming aspects of American society in recent years. Given the traditions of individualism, populism, "debunking," and even of conspiracy, large sections of the populace have often been wary of government. Yet, from a low point during the Depression, generalized trust in the society began to rise, so that in the 1950s, 80 percent of the people said they trusted the government. The mood began to turn during the Vietnam War, and sank to a low of 33 percent in 1976! On more specific questions, the figures were even more startling. The number of individuals who stated that "the government" wastes a lot of money

rose from 43 percent in 1958 to 78 percent in 1980. Those who said "you cannot trust the government to do right most of the time" went from 23 percent in 1958 to 73 percent in 1980. The rising level of mistrust, particularly between 1976 and 1978, led President Jimmy Carter to make his famous speech about the "malaise" in American society, in 1979. See, S. M. Lipset and William Schneider, *The Confidence Gap* (New York: The Free Press, 1983), pp. 13–18.

31. On the interim figures, see S. M. Lipset, *The Economy, Elections and Public Opinion,* Hoover Institution Working Paper P-83-1 (July 1983), pp. 1–3. Ms. Lynch's statement was published in *Business Week* (November 19, 1984), p. 37.

32. Mr. Vigurie wrote

The 1984 Reagan campaign, run from the White House by the chief of staff, James A. Baker 3rd, will rank among the all-time greatest blunders in American politics.

Framed by "feel good" television commercials that helped Democratic incumbents as well as Republicans ("re-elect everybody" was the unintended message), the campaign was a disaster for loyal Reagan supporters running on the G.O.P. ticket for Congress. Not since the Eisenhower and Nixon reelection campaigns have lower-level candidates been double-crossed to such a degree by the President's campaign managers. . . .

Mr. Baker . . . could have used hard-edged, issue-oriented commercials to make the election a referendum on Reagan-style conservatism, but [he] didn't. [He] could have sent Mr. Reagan into areas where he could have helped struggling G.O.P. candidates, but [he] didn't, except for a few poorly planned trips in the last eight days.

The House minority leader, Robert H. Michel of Illinois, echoes the sentiments of Republicans across the country when he blamed Mr. Reagan for the disappointing showing in the House because 'he never really, in my opinion, joined that issue of what it really means to have the numbers in the House.' He said: "Here the son of a buck ended up with 59 percent and you bring in [only] 15 seats."

33. I have based my description of the demographic change in the U.S. on the analysis of David Broder published in his *Boston Globe* column after the election, November 11, 1984.

34. Martin P. Wattenberg, *The Decline of American Political Parties* (Cambridge, Mass.: Harvard University Press, 1983).

35. In this respect, it is striking to look at previous "landslides" comparable to that of Mr. Reagan. In 1964, Lyndon Johnson won 61 percent of the popular vote and 90.3 percent of the electoral vote,

while in 1972 Richard Nixon won 60.7 percent of the popular vote and 96.7 percent of the electoral vote. One explanation has been that in both cases, the "center" won against the "extremes"; in the one instance, this was brought about by the fear of Barry Goldwater, in the other of George McGovern. Yet, Stanley Kelley, Jr. points out that Johnson won because of his projection of competence and a positive image, while Richard Nixon was regarded largely as "the lesser of two evils." Thus the personality of the man, rather than the issues, was decisive in the election. Stanley Kelly, *Interpreting Elections* (Princeton, N.J.: Princeton University Press, 1984).

36. *The Politics of Aristotle,* edited by Ernest Barker (Oxford: The Clarendon Press, 1948), p. 261. (Book VI, Ch. 3, #3, 1318a for citation to other editions.)

37. "The Combined Effects of Major Changes in Federal Taxes and Spending Programs Since 1981," Staff Memorandum, Congressional Budget Office (April, 1984), p. 7. (The memorandum was prepared at the request of Senator Lawron Chiles, ranking minority member of the Senate Budget Committee.)

38. "Financial Markets and Monetary Economics," *NBER Reporter* (Summer 1984). (Emphasis added.)

39. Alan S. Blinder and Douglas Holtz-Eakin, "Public Opinion and the Balanced Budget," *American Economic Review,* -74 (May, 1984).

40. When President Reagan signed the Deficit Reduction Act, the "down payment" to raise $49 billion over three years, Senator Dole, the chairman of the Senate Finance Committee, slipped in a $170 million break for gasohol and alcohol, made with grain raised by his Kansas constituents. Dan Rostenkowski, of Chicago, the chairman of the House Ways and Means Committee, blocked a Treasury effort to collect $300 million in back taxes on "straddle transactions," from the commodity exchanges in Chicago.

41. Charls E. Walker, Undersecretary of the Treasury in the Nixon administration, declared soon after: "Many instant historians saw the forced resignation of Richard Nixon as the 93rd Congress's long-term claim to fame. We disagree. Our nomination is the Budget Reform Act of 1974, which established an orderly and rational Congressional budget procedure." *The New York Times* (July 13, 1984.)

42. "The result is," Alice Rivlin writes, "that the Budget Appendix is as long and as readable as the Manhattan phone directory. Authorization, appropriation and tax bills are voluminous and com-

plicated. Nor is the preoccupation with minutiae confined to author-izing, appropriation and tax committees. Debate on the budget res-olution . . . often ends up focussing on detailed concerns about protecting very specific programs." Alice Rivlin, "Reform of the Budget Process," *American Economic Review* (May 1984), pp. 134–135. For an earlier assessment, see "The Political Economy of Bud-get Choices: A View from Congress," *American Economic Review* (May 1981).

43. From an interview with James Reston, *New York Times* (April 12, 1984).

44. *Reducing the Deficit: Spending and Revenue Options* (Wash-ington, D.C.: Congressional Budget Office, February, 1984), Part III, p. 91.

45. I leave aside, as outside my purview, the question of the de-fense budget in part because the administration has ruled this off bounds, and it therefore becomes, like the interest costs on the debt, a binding constraint which reduces the freedom of maneuver for all other options and, in part, because the Pentagon budget is itself so arcane that few outsiders can master it. I call attention to a study by William W. Kaufman , *The 1985 Defense Budget* (Washington, D.C.: Brookings Institution, 1984). As *The New York Times* quoted Pro-fessor Kaufmann,

In the last three years . . . accounts in the Pentagon budget dealing with procurement, research and development, and military construction have risen 86 percent, but accounts associated with operation and support of the military have risen only 30 percent. The implication is that the Pentagon may soon not be able to afford to use all the new, complex weapons it is buying.

Mr. Kaufmann also presses the point that because of the rate at which mili-tary appropriations have grown, large backlogs of spending authority have been created that will be difficult for Congress to control in the future.

"Even if Congress holds the fiscal 1985 defense budget to the neighborhood of $290 billion in budget authority," he writes, "expenditures from the backlog will come to more than $110 billion by fiscal 1986."

A result, he says, will be that more than one-third of military outlays will be "committed and uncontrollable" even before Congress takes action on the budget for that year.

Mr. Kaufmann goes on to suggest a 1985 Pentagon budget of about $260 billion, as against the $305 billion originally proposed by President Reagan.

(*The New York Times* [April 19, 1984], p. .)

46. Herbert Stein, in his book *Presidential Economics,* indicates the problems of this reasoning. As James Fallows reports Stein's example: "Stein gives an estimate of a 30 percent across-the-board cut in tax rates, the original goal of the Kemp-Roth bill. For a doctor earning $120,000 a year, this would mean a reduction of $12,000 in his tax bill; for someone earning $25,000 a reduction of about $1,000. If the tax cut were to pay for itself, the doctor would have to respond to the attractive new incentives by working nearly 30 percent more hours than before, and the other man would have to work 20 percent more than he used to. Some people might do so, but would everyone, or even most?" *New York Review of Books* (April 12, 1984), p. 10.

47. *Federal Support of U.S. Business* (Washington, D.C.: Congressional Budget Office, January 1984), Summary Table, page x.

48. Arend Lijphart, *Democracies: Patterns of Majoritarian and Consensus Government in Twenty-One Countries* (Yale University Press, 1984).

49. Albert Hirschman, *The Passions and the Interests: Political Arguments for Capitalism Before Its Triumph* (Princeton, N.J.: Princeton University Press, 1974).

BUDGET DEFICITS

Lester Thurow
Gordon Y Billard
Professor of Economics and Management
Massachusetts Institute of Technology

Budget Deficits

Persistent large budget deficits lead to four problems. Each is serious but none shows up as a sudden cirsis requiring immediate attention. If democracies require crises to move them to solve problems, then large budget deficits would be among the most conducive to force democracies to find some solution. However, they never generate the sudden widespread perception that society must pull together and sacrifice to solve a common problem.

1. Less Investment

Large budget deficits usually represent negative savings. Funds must be borrowed from the pool of savings that would otherwise be used to finance private investment to finance public expenditures. If these public expenditures are for consumption purposes, then budget deficits represent a direct transfer from investment to consumption. Currently, the deficit of the U.S. government is almost entirely the result of financing public consumption; the major expenditures are made for national defense and social security or medicare. The public investment part of the federal budget is shrinking. Such a transfer from investment to consumption slows any country's long-run rate of growth and leads its productivity, international competitiveness, and standard of living to fall relative to those countries who are saving and investing more. From this perspective large budget deficits are more serious in the United States than they would be for many other industrial countries. Since the United States saves less, large public deficits simply eat up a greater fraction of total savings in the United States than they would elsewhere.

In 1983 the United States invested 10.5 percent of its GNP in plant and equipment and 3.9 percent of its GNP in housing. This puts us far below our competitors. In 1982 American investment was less than half that of Japan and 25 percent below that of most other industrial countries (see Table 1).[1] Even in a boom year such as

Table 1. Gross Fixed Capital Formation[a]

Country	1978	1982
United States	18.1	14.5
Italy	18.8	19.2
Germany	21.5	20.5
Japan	30.2	29.6
France	21.5	20.9
Canada	25.7	21.9
United Kingdom	18.1	15.4

[a]Percent of GNP.

1978, American investment was substantially below that of its competitors. As a result, workers in the rest of the world are increasingly working with better plant and equipment than workers in the United States.

In the four years of the Carter administration, personal savings were 4.1 percent of the GNP and the federal deficit absorbed 1.7 percent of the GNP. If the negative savings of the federal government is added to personal savings, only 2.4 percent of the GNP was available to augment business saving and to finance housing investments under President Carter.[2] This was, and is, inadequate.

When housing investment is subtracted from personal savings, there is very little left to finance business investment even when the government is running a balanced budget. In 1983 individuals saved $113 billion but spent $131 billion on residential investment.[3] Instead of households helping finance industry, businesses helped to finance housing.

But in 1983 with the tax cuts fully in place, personal savings were down to 3.4 percent of the GNP. With lower tax rates and higher defense spending the federal deficit had risen to 5.5 percent of the GNP. Instead of augmenting business savings, persons and government were subtracting 2.2 percent from business savings in 1983.[4] No country can compete and grow under such circumstances.

Not surprisingly, the real cost of capital is lower abroad where there are more savings to be borrowed. With a lower cost of capital, potential investments that conform to desired foreign rates of return on investment do not meet necessarily higher American rates. The rest of the industrial world can afford to work with equipment that Americans cannot afford to use.

Historically American firms reduced the personal savings deficiency in the U.S. by saving more than their foreign counterparts. In 1983 businesses saved $455 billion or 13.7 percent of the GNP in the form of undistributed profits and capital consumption allowances.[5] This exceeded the same year's $341 billion in nonresidential-business investment. American industry essentially ended up providing all of its own savings, financing a portion of housing investments, and underwriting a part of the government deficit. Such a system cannot continue. It provides too little savings for business investment now and is apt to provide even less in the future. Higher American business savings rates were produced by higher profit rates and these in turn were produced by a technological lead that is disappearing. Competitors are driving down American profit rates and in the future will be depressing business savings.

In a competitive world one has to save and invest as much as one's most agressive competitor. This means American savings rates in the long-run must be high enough to compete with Japan. But Japan is still behind the United States in terms of per capita GNP and productivity. As a result, it is not yet necessary to keep up with the Japanese. It is, however, necessary to keep up with the investment rates in the European countries that are already equal to or maybe even slightly ahead of us if we are to keep them from widening the current productivity gap. Since America's work force is growing more rapidly than Europe's work force to keep capital-labor ratios growing at the same rate, investment in the U.S. will have to be somewhat higher than it is in Europe.

In 1982 Americans invested 11 percent of the GNP in industrial plant and equipment. Given potential hours of work growing at 4 percent per year, America has to invest 13 percent of the GNP just to keep its capital-labor ratio constant. To keep our capital-labor ratio growing at the European rate would have required an investment of 20 percent of the GNP in 1982. And if we want to invest a normal amount in housing, another 5 percent of the GNP would have to be invested for an aggregate investment rate of 25 percent. *As a result, America should set itself the goal of increasing gross fixed investment to 25 percent of the GNP.* To do this will require actions to raise personal savings rates (a subject not covered in this paper), but it will also require the federal government to shift from being a large dissaver to being a large saver.

2. Inflationary Pressures

Large budget deficits were appropriate in the midst of the Great Depression or the recession of 1981 and 1982, but they become inappropriate as an economy recovers and returns to full employment. Eventually, budget deficits represent too large an infusion of aggregate demand and inflation results.

It is important to remember, however, that generalized excess aggregate demand has a very different impact on inflation than that resulting from a supply shock. Where supply shocks lead to sudden, sharp, localized inflationary pressures, excess aggregate demand leads to slow, persistent, and very widespread inflationary pressures. In the Viet Nam War period America injected too much aggregate demand into the economy, but inflation only slowly accelerated from 2.2 percent in 1965 to 5.4 percent in 1970 (using the GNP deflator). Five years were necessary to raise the inflation rate by 3 percentage points. Given the current degree of idle capacity, people, and equipment, one can easily imagine the current president making it through his term of office until January 1989 without inflation reaching the point that it would be considered a crisis and demand attention.

From a Keynesian perspective, budget deficits should be eliminated as the economy approaches full employment if inflation is to be avoided. And the higher one places the natural rate of unemployment (the rate of unemployment at which inflation starts to accelerate), the faster the budget deficit must be eliminated. Those who believe that the natural rate of unemployment is 7.5 percent need a balanced budget now. Those who believe that the natural rate of unemployment is 4 percent do not need a balanced budget for a while.

3. Fighting Future Recessions

Even with a large budget deficit a recession is not impossible. Such a recession could be produced, for example, by a balance-of-trade deficit larger than the deficit in the federal budget. The federal budget would be injecting aggregate demand into the system but the trade deficit would be subtracting aggregate demand in even larger amounts.

As America has just demonstrated, federal deficits are the appropriate remedy for recessions. If the federal deficit is already very large, however, public policy makers are much less likely to pursue vigorously such deficit policies at the appropriate time. Europe is having a weak recovery from the recession of 1981 and 1982 in large part because European countries felt that they could not enlarge their already large budget deficits. Without the American trade deficit as an external injection of aggregate demand, Europe would still be stuck in the recession that began in 1981.

As a practical political matter, to inject massive amounts of aggregate demand into a stalled economy it is necessary to start from a position of equilibrium in the federal budget. If such a starting point is not reached during full-employment periods, recessions will be sharper and longer than they otherwise would be.

4. International Competitiveness

In the long run, international competitiveness depends upon productivity growth; in the short run, it can be directly affected by federal budget deficits. Given a smaller pool of savings, simple supply and demand leads to higher real-interest rates in the United States that would occur if the federal budget was not in deficit.

But higher interest rates are of interest to foreign savers as well as American savers. Seeking to get high American interest rates, foreign savers move funds into the United States. This, in the short run, alleviates the savings shortage in the United States, but it also serves to drive up the value of the dollar and make American firms noncompetitive on world markets. Because capital inflows lead to an overvalued dollar, America's trade deficit is approaching $130 billion in 1984. Such a trade deficit helps on the inflationary front (American firms cannot raise prices because of low-cost foreign competitors), but it also represents the loss of 3 million American jobs.

In the short run, American firms lose in the market

share here and abroad, but more importantly some long-run damage is done to America's competitive position. Foreign firms build up service networks, develop customer loyalty, and make high profits which they can devote to developing new products and processes. When the dollar goes down, American firms will find it difficult to recapture many of the markets which they have lost during the period of overvaluation.

No country can forever run a large deficit in its balance of payments. Even if the American fiscal and monetary policies are never shifted toward smaller budget deficits and lower interest rates, the dollar will eventually fall. Eventually the rest of the world will conclude that they have enough of their liquid assets invested in America and will quit investing more. When this happens the dollar falls.

A falling dollar presents Americans with a mixture of positives and negatives. The 3 million lost jobs are gradually transferred back to the United States, but the falling dollar also constitutes an inflationary shock. If the dollar is 30 to 35 percent overvalued (the standard estimate), then a declining dollar will add directly 3.5 percentage points of inflation to an economy that imports about 10 percent of its GNP. In addition there will be an indirect inflationary shock as those firms who compete with imports and cannot now raise their prices (autos?) do so. This indirect shock will be as large as the direct shock. Together the direct and indirect effects of a falling dollar can easily bring America back to double-digit inflation.

By running a large federal deficit after it was appropriate to do so, the American government has created a future inflationary shock for itself.

It is Not a Problem

Those who argue that large federal deficits are not a problem make several arguments that need to be examined in detail to understand why those arguments are incorrect.

1. It is argued that if government deficits (state, local, and federal) are compared with those of our major international competitors, our deficits are not much larger than theirs.

True but irrelevant.

Since our major industrial competitors save much more than we save, they can run deficits as large as ours with much less adverse impact on investment. Americans now invest less and simply cannot afford any further reduction in relative investment springing from the absorption of private savings in a public sector deficit.

State and local governments save money in the United States (they are more or less required to do so in the funding of their pension programs), but they have been saving for more than a decade and their saving is already counted in national savings. Without their saving, national savings and investment would be much lower than it is. State and local governments are not a new source of national savings that can be used to offset new federal deficits.

2. It is argued that America is borrowing much of the needed funds from abroad and that therefore the federal deficits have not been crowding out private investment.

True in the past, but unlikely to be true in the future.

In 1983 and 1984 much of the negative impact of savings on the federal budget has been offset by borrowing funds from abroad. But this is a process that cannot long continue. As has been mentioned, at any given real-interest rate there is a finite share of their assets that foreigners wish to hold in the United States. To maintain net foreign lending, U.S. real-interest rates have to be raised continually relative to those of the rest of the industrial world. This cannot occur, and, if it were to occur, it would make new investment in plant and equipment in America impossible. Demanded real rates of return would be so high that few projects could earn what would have to be earned.

If the lending were to continue, the United States would also gradually become a net debtor nation in the same sense that Mexico and Brazil are now net debtor nations. As they have found out and we would find out, eventually the time comes when the rest of the world wants to be paid back for what they have lent in the past. At this time the average American standard of living would have to fall to release the goods and services that foreigners want in repayment of their debts. The per capita Brazilian income has fallen, for example, by about 11 percent.

Foreign borrowing is one of the few ways that it really is possible for one generation of Americans to place an economic burden of a later generation of Americans. In 1984 Americans were consuming $130 billion more than they were producing, and, at some time in the future, Americans will have to produce $130 billion more than their are consuming to repay the international debts incurred to finance 1984's trade deficit.

3. It is argued that America can grow its way out of the deficit.

Not true.

When it comes to growing our way out of the deficit, the basic problem is arithmetic. Yes, it is possible for the United States to grow its way out of the current deficit, but to do so would require such low unemployment rates and such an improvement in productivity growth that it is highly unlikely.

Expressed as a fraction of the GNP, the federal government has a marginal tax-collection and benefit-reduction propensity of about 24 percent. Every $1 increase in the GNP yields the federal government an extra 24 cents in budget deficit reduction. This means that if the 1984 Federal deficit (about $165 billion) were to have been eliminated with economic growth, the economy would have had to have been 18.7 percent of $688 billion bigger than it was. Since expenditure programs are growing just about as fast as revenue, this is the growth gap that must be closed if growth is to solve the problem.

Suppose that growth were to be used to bring about a balanced budget by 1990. If unemployment could be reduced from 7.5 percent to 3.5 percent without causing inflation (something few people think possible), then four percentage points of the necessary GNP gap could be eliminated by simply operating the economy at a higher level of capacity utilization. But this would still leave 14.7 percentage points of growth gap, however, that would have to be eliminated with productivity growth higher than that now underlying budget projects. Spread out over five years, productivity growth would have to accelerate by approximately 3 percentage points per year. Instead of the 1.6 percent per year productivity growth underlying the high and rising federal deficit forecast by outsiders such as Data Resources, Inc., productivity would have to grow at 4.6 percent.

Since World War II the United States has never had a five-year period of time when productivity growth was as high as it is now. In the five years from 1978 to 1983 productivity grew at 1.1 percent per year. In a recovery cyclical productivity automatically rebounds as overhead labor is spread across more units of output. Because of this, productivity grew at 2.7 percent in 1983— a big improvement over 1.1 percent but still far below the required 4.6 percent. And by the third quarter of 1984 productivity growth had entirely stopped in the nonfarm business sector of the economy.

Given both history and current events, the necessary underlying rate of growth of productivity for growing America's way out of its budget deficit simply is not there.

Cutting Expenditures and Raising Taxes

If the budget-deficit problem is serious (it is) and cannot be solved with the passage of time (it cannot), attention must be focused on either raising taxes or cutting expenditures. Either of these options could cause a serious problem. As taxes and expenditures are now structured it simply is not possible to raise the necessary revenue with surtaxes or across-the-board expenditure cuts. The structure of the current system simply is not strong enough to absorb what must be absorbed.

Consider the federal income tax as an example. If the projected 1985 federal deficit were to be eliminated with an income-tax surcharge, the surtax would have to be levied at a 55 percent rate. Everyone understands that if the current system were to be maintained, taxpayers instructed to calculate their taxes, and then made to add 55 percent to their tax payments, the whole system would explode.

To do what must be done—to impose a combination of tax increases and expenditure cuts—is going to require some fundamental changes in the nature of the tax system and in many of our expenditure programs. Taxes and expenditures are going to have to be rethought and restructured.

Raising Taxes

The Corporate Income Tax

While Americans often talk as if corporations pay taxes, and they do write checks to the government, corporations cannot pay taxes. Taxes are paid by some combination of (1) the owners of the corporation, who receive lower dividends because some of their profits are taken in taxes, (2) the customers of corporations, who must pay higher prices because taxes are included as an extra cost in the prices of what they buy, or (3) the employees of corporations, who receive lower wages because their employer has less after-tax income to pay them.

The economics literature on tax incidence disagrees as to where the actual short-run burden lies, but in the long run the tax must be shifted forward onto the consumer in the form of higher prices. Savers demand an after-tax rate of return on their savings equal to the rate at which they are willing to trade consumption today for consumption tomorrow. A person who is willing to give up one dollar in consumption today for an extra $1.10 in consumption a year from now demands an after-tax return of 10 percent. If he does not get it, he will simply consume his dollar today and not save. As this occurs, the capital available for investment falls, driving up the cost of capital and leading to higher production costs and higher prices for consumption goods—shifting the incidence of the tax forward onto the consumer. With less capital but a higher pretax rate of return to capital, the after-tax rate of return on capital is gradually restored, eliminating the corporate shareholder as a real taxpayer.

As a result, efforts to tax the rich by taxing corporate income are ultimately self-defeating. What looks like a tax on wealthy corporate shareholders is in fact a disguised sales tax.

Moreover, even if the corporate income tax were paid by shareholders, it is an unfair tax. Every shareholder, rich or poor, is taxed at the same rate, about 46 percent. There are much better, fairer ways than the corporate income tax to tax the rich.

Whatever the merits or demerits of an efficient corporate income tax, however, they have little to do with our actual inefficient corporate income tax. An efficient corporate income tax would raise revenue with the fewest possible distortions—the pattern of investments with the tax should be similar to the pattern of investments without the tax. Yet, America has created a monster of a corporate income tax with enormous distortions. The distortions are so large that if the current system were allowed to continue it would burden the economy with such an inefficient pattern of investments that it would severely handicap America's efforts to compete with the rest of the world.

The problems have been growing for a number of decades but were vastly magnified with the tax changes enacted by the Reagan administration in 1981. One problem is that of revenue. In 1950 the corporate income tax yielded 25 percent of the revenue raised by the federal government but by 1986 the corporate income tax will raise only 7 percent of the Federal revenue.[6] The corporate income tax is gradually being eliminated, but we are failing to fill the revenue gap left behind. If we want to abolish the corporate income tax, we are going to have to be willing to pay for it with some other form of taxation.

But the problems extend far beyond those of too little revenue. In 1981 the Reagan administration enacted what is now called the Accelerated Cost Recovery System (ACRS). Essentially ACRS is a system of accelerated depreciation allowances; that is, an investment may be depreciated in a much shorter length of time than that in which the investment will actually be used.

If the period of depreciation is short enough relative to the actual length of life of an asset, effective corporate tax rates can be reduced to zero or even to negative rates—in effect a subsidy. Suppose, for example, that you invest in a machine that costs $1 million and will last ten years. The machine earns $100,000 per year after all expenses (including the $100,000 per year that must be set aside to replace the machine when it wears out or to repay the loan) have been paid. If you borrowed the $1 million and were paying a 10 percent interest rate, no taxes would be owed on the $100,000 in annual earnings since they are given to your lender, and, as interest payments, they are tax deductible. With economic depreciation no taxes would be owed on the $100,000 per year set aside to replace the machine or repay the loan. As a result this project just breaks even. It repays the lender but there is nothing left over.

Now, suppose that the government allows a 10 percent investment tax credit on new investment and permits the same machine to be depreciated into two years rather than its ten years of actual life. The $100,000 in annual earnings is still a tax-free interest deduction. But the investor now gets a $100,000 tax credit and a $500,000 deduction from taxes in each of the first two years. If the investor has other taxable income, these deductions can be used to shelter it. The two years of depreciation deductions are together worth $955,000 in net present value (the number is not $1 million since today's value of $500,000 one year from now is $455,000 with 10 percent interest rates) and the investment tax credit another $100,000. If the investor puts his $1,055,000 in tax-free income to work at 10 percent, he will have $2.7 million at the end of ten years. He repays the $1 million loan and is left with a profit of $1.7 million. What was a breakeven project is now a very profitable project.

Such a subsidy system certainly encourages more investment, but it also induces investors to misallocate capital because they can now make money on projects that do not earn the competitive (10 percent) market rate of return.[7] What is worse, if the length of time over which an asset can be depreciated relative to its actual useful economic life differs for different types of assets, the tax system offers very different subsidies for different kinds of investment.

Reagan's ACRS, for example, allows a larger subsidy for long-lived assets such as steel mills than for short-lived assets such as equipment in an electronics factory. The result is an incentive to invest in too many steel mills and not enough electronics equipment. The pattern of investment is distorted away from those very activities that would have the greatest output enhancing potential.

ACRS also distorts incentives between profitable companies and unprofitable companies—which is often the same as the distinction between new and old companies. Tax credits and tax deductions have no value unless you have taxable income. As a result, if General Motors is profitable and Ford is not, General Motors but not Ford gets the subsidies implicit in ACRS. Similarly new, rapidly investing firms are unlikely to have enough income to use their allowable credits and deductions. In contrast, a stagnant, noninvesting firm with a substantial cash flow can use its tax credits and end up paying lower taxes than the new progressive firm. This makes it harder for the new dynamic firms to make market inroads on old stagnant firms.

To cure these problems the Reagan administration enacted lease backs along with the ACRS system in 1981. Lease backs were basically a way for sick firms or new firms to seel their unused tax breaks. Thus, in 1981 the Ford Motor Company sold a significant fraction of its unusable tax subsidies to IBM. In the market that developed for tax breaks the seller usually got about 90 cents for every dollar of tax reduction gained by the buyer. Ford got 90 percent of the tax breaks it would have gotten if it had been profitable and IBM was able to reduce its tax bill by 10 percent.

But in the process of solving one problem, this legislation created others. Firms with taxable profits such as IBM were not paying taxes to the federal government but were essentially paying taxes to another private firm, Ford. Efficient profitable firms ended up subsidizing inefficient firms. The resulting furor led to the 1982 repeal of lease backs, but nothing else was done to solve the problems which lease backs were designed to solve. The distortions lease backs were designed to cure in ACRS were once again back in force.

Without lease backs, ACRS generates long-run tax

incentives for mergers and acquisitions. Profitable firms buy up unprofitable firms with large unuseable tax credits, use the tax credits, and then sell off the firm that has just been acquired. While there is nothing intrinsically wrong with mergers and takeovers, everything is wrong with mergers and takeovers that are done solely for tax reasons. Time, effort, and money go into a sophisticated system of tax avoidance rather than into producing a better, cheaper product.

Given the likelihood that the corporate income tax is in fact a regressive consumption tax, the national need for investment incentives, the small amount of revenue that will be collected under current laws, the huge legal and bookkeeping costs of administering the present system, and the mess created by ACRS, the corporate income tax should be abolished. There are simply better, fairer, more efficient ways to raise the revenue that the federal government must raise.

The Payroll Tax

While the corporate income tax has gradually diminished, the payroll tax has been growing from 12 to 35 percent of federal revenue.[8] Social-Security and unemployment-insurance payroll taxes together now exceed 16 percent of payroll and will be well above 20 percent before the turn of the century. Current laws also understate the increase that will be required. Within months of the 1983 tax increase which was supposed to solve Social Security financing problems for the rest of the century, discussions had started as to how to raise the revenue necessary to finance Medicare. Unemployment insurance is a federally mandated system dependent upon payroll taxes that is clearly underfunded. More than half the states ran out of funds in the early 1980s and were borrowing funds from the federal government to pay unemployment insurance benefits. At some point, payroll taxes are going to have to be raised to repay those loans and to pay future benefits.

Liberals traditionally object to payroll taxes on the grounds that taxes paid go down as a fraction of total income as incomes go up since payroll taxes are not levied on all of earned income or on income from investments. It is misleading, however, to look solely at taxes when they are paid into a trust fund and used to finance a particular set of expenditures. One must look at both taxes and expenditures together before equity judgments can be drawn. If expenditures are distributed so that low-income individuals get more benefits than upper-income individuals, a progressive expenditure pattern can more than offset a regressive tax pattern. And this is the case in both Social-Security and unemployment insurance. Because of the minimum monthly benefit the ratio of benefits to taxes is higher for low income individuals than it is for high income individuals in Social Security. Similarly in unemployment insurance the greatest benefits go to those with the highest probabilities of being unemployed. Since the probability of being unemployed goes up as one's income goes down, unemployment insurance is also a system where a progressive benefit structure more than offsets a regressive tax structure.

The real objection to payroll taxes is not equity, but efficiency. They provide an incentive for employers to reduce employment. Payroll taxes raise the costs of hiring labor and thus create an extra incentive to reduce costs by substituting machines that do not have to pay payroll taxes. The effect is most dramatic in the case of a firm deciding whether it is most profitable to hire a robot or a worker. If it hires a robot, it pays no payroll taxes. If it hires a human worker, it pays an extra 16 percent in payroll taxes. Not only does the robot not have to pay a payroll tax, the purchase may lead to an actual tax subsidy via the accelerated cost-recovery system. The government ends up paying firms to use robots and charging firms if they use human workers. If such distortions are to be prevented, the payroll tax should be reduced and not used to finance future increases in social insurance benefits.

The Value-added Tax

To ask what tax could possibly be raised to yield such a large sum of revenue is to come up with one and only one answer—the value-added tax. Value-added taxes, common in the rest of the industrial world, are determined by subtracting a firm's purchases of materials or components from its gross selling revenue and levying a tax upon the difference—the firm's value added. If a firm bought supplies worth $10 million and sold products worth $18 million dollars, it would have a value added of $8 million. With a 10 percent value-added tax, the firm would owe $800,000 in value-added taxes. These taxes would be built into the prices of what the firm sells.

Value-added taxes are widely used abroad because they raise large amounts of money while simultaneously creating incentives to consume less and save more. Instead of being taxed upon what one puts into society (the income from work and savings) one is taxed on the consumption one takes out of society. With a 15 percent value-added tax, a person who buys a $10,000 car must pay an extra $1,500 in value-added taxes when he buys the car but can completely avoid those taxes if he instead saves the $10,000. As a result, the incentive effects of value-added taxes work in favor of what society wants, less consumption, rather than against what society wants, more savings and work, as is the case with higher personal income taxes. As a result value-added taxes are an integral part of any program seeking to encourage more private saving and to transform government from a dissaver into a saver.

Value-added taxes also make it possible to tax illegal underground activity that is not now taxed. The Florida drug smuggler may pay no taxes when he sells his cocaine, but must pay the value-added tax when he buys his Mercedes. Millions of Americans who are illegally evading income taxes would be caught when they spend their income. The greater a country's problems with tax compliance, the more imperative the value added tax becomes.

The value-added tax is also self-enforcing. To cheat on the value-added tax, a firm must under-invoice its sales or over-invoice its purchases of materials to reduce its value added. If sales are under-invoiced a firm's customers have fewer purchases of materials which they can subtract from their sales revenues, and they must pay more taxes on a larger value added. If purchases are over-invoiced then a firm's suppliers have larger sales, a higher value added, and must pay more taxes. While a firm may try to cheat either its suppliers or its customers so that they have to pay more taxes, the government is not left without its rightful revenue.

The value-added tax also has an advantage in international trade. The value-added tax is rebatable under the rules of international trade where other taxes are not.

Thus, when Germany exports a car to the United States, German car companies get a tax refund, say $2,000, from their government. When German cars are exported to Japan this refund makes no difference since Japan also uses value-added taxes and the German car exporter will have to pay $2,000 in value-added taxes when the car arrives in Japan. But it makes a difference when the car is exported to a country like the United States which does not have value-added taxes. The rebate is still given but there is no countervailing levy that must be paid. German companies are essentially selling cars that do not have to carry a tax burden when they are sold in the United States.

When an American company exports a car it cannot get a $2,000 refund for the corporate income or payroll taxes which it pays; it also must pay the foreign value-added tax. American cars sold abroad essentially pay two sets of taxes. This creates a $2,000 handicap for American car manufacturers in export markets and a $2,000 advantage to foreign car manufacturers in the United States. The only solution is to establish a value-added tax as large as that used in the rest of the industrial world.

While Sweden has a 25 percent value-added tax, America could probably get by with the 15 to 20 percent that is common in most of the rest of Europe. In 1982 a 15 percent value-added tax would have raised $412 billion in America.[9]

Since the value-added tax is essentially levied upon consumption and consumption falls as a fraction of income as incomes rise, the tax payments fall as a fraction of total income as incomes rise. Fortunately there is an easy way to convert a regressive value-added tax into a progressive one. The value-added tax is levied at some flat rate on all goods and services, but a per-capita refundable tax credit is given to offset the effects of the tax on the poor. Suppose, for example, that we had a 15 percent value-added tax and a refundable per-capita tax credit of $375. A family of four with an income of $10,000 (approximately the poverty line) would pay $1,500 in value-added taxes when it spent its income but get that $1,500 (4 × $375) back in the form of a refund. On a net basis it would not be paying the value-added tax at all. A four-person family spending $20,000 would pay $3,000, get a $1,500 refund, and pay a net value-added tax of $1,500. Similarly, a four-person family spending $50,000 would pay $7,500, get the $1,500 back, and be a net payer of $6,000. And so on up the income ladder. Such a system of refundable credits can be used to make the value-added tax as progressive as anyone desires.

By integrating the refunds into income-tax withholding tables, the rebate can be effectively returned to the taxpayer as it is paid. A large rebate also forces the millions of people who now evade taxes by simply not filing the necessary forms to file. Unless they filed they would not get their rebate. As a result, income-tax compliance would go up.

If America had had a 15 percent value-added tax with a $375 refundable tax credit in 1982, $87 billion would have been refunded in credits and the value-added tax would have raised $325 billion on a net basis. This would have been enough to finance the elimination of the corporate income tax, the reduction of the payroll tax, the elimination of the deficit, and still generate a substantial surplus.

Since value-added taxes are included in the prices of the products we buy, any increase in the value-added tax shows up in inflation as it is usually measured. If wages or other prices are indexed to the measured rate of inflation (a common situation in labor-union contracts and in contracts with suppliers), higher value-added taxes cause higher wages or prices and hence even higher inflation than the value-added tax would have warranted by itself. In Britain in the late 1970s Mrs. Thatcher forgot about this effect—to her regret. She enacted a major increase in the value-added tax and then saw it show up as a huge increase in the rate of inflation as wages and prices rose in a sickening spiral.

When the value-added tax is designed to replace two other taxes (the payroll and corporate income tax) that also raise the costs of production there should be no big inflationary effect, but, whatever the size of the effect, it should be kept out of the cost-of-living indexes. This easily can be and should be done by those constructing the index. If taxes are to be included in cost-of-living indexes, then it is necessary to include the value of government goods and services received since taxes are used to buy government goods and services. A cost-of-living index should either include all taxes and government benefits or no taxes and benefits. Since the existing cost-of-living index includes neither income taxes nor government benefits, the index should not include other forms of taxation either.

Converting the Personal Income Tax into a Personal Consumption Tax

The truth about the federal personal income tax is not that it is on average progressive or regressive, but that it is unfair. Some people with high incomes pay high taxes; others pay low taxes.[10] Several hundred Ameri-

cans with incomes over \$1 million per year pay little or
no tax, yet there are high income Americans who pay
the full amount.

Hoping to conserve energy, help charities, promote
investments in cattle, and thousands of other things the
federal personal income-tax system has acquired so many
legal loopholes that it is like cheap Swiss cheese—more
holes than cheese.[11] Most of these loopholes benefit
investors (rich or poor) and not wage earners (rich or
poor), but almost everyone ends up with a few dollars
worth of loopholes. The result is a structure of legal
loopholes that favors the rich on average but is very hard
to alter since most of us are beneficiaries of at least a
few dollars worth of loopholes.

The problem with such a system is not just that it un-
fairly assesses different taxes on individuals with the same
income, but that it set up a corrosive social system. The
average citizen without loopholes sees President Nixon
paying no taxes because of special legal loopholes for
gifts of personal papers to libraries (this loophole has now
been closed). If the "big guys" can give themselves legal loopholes, the average citizen thinks that he will build
himself some illegal loopholes. Voluntary compliance
deteriorates. The U.S. Treasury estimates that it loses
almost more in illegal tax evasion, \$85 billion, as it does
in legal loopholes, \$65 billion.[12]

No tax system can work without honest voluntary
compliance on the part of the vast majority of citizens.
The Internal Revenue Service can collect taxes from the
dishonest few, but it cannot collect taxes from a dishonest majority or even a large minority. In 1983 the Internal Revenue Services attempted impose withholding on
interest and dividend payments to help them collect the
billions of dollars that they should have been collecting

but were not. Since most interest payments are left in bank accounts the IRS's efforts were defeated by the banks who did not want funds withdrawn from their accounts. Yet, it is simply a physical impossibility for the Internal Revenue Service to track down millions of tax cheaters.

Every dishonest taxpayer essentially raises the taxes that must be paid by the honest, and wage earners eventually begin to see themselves as "suckers" paying what others should be paying. Wage earners begin cheating to match the cheating of those who should be paying on interest and dividends by telling their employer that they have 15 children so that he does not withhold from their earnings, and then they fail to file an income tax form. As long as millions are doing it, and 15 million people are doing it, the chances of getting caught are very small. When this happens, it is only a matter of time until the tax system collapses. No society can long run without an efficient, fair way to collect the revenue that it needs to operate. Both the perception and reality of fairness are necessary because without them there is no efficient way to collect taxes from a hostile noncooperative citizenry.

The Bradley-Gephart bill is the current embodiment of the old liberal dreams of tax reforms designed to close most loopholes and restore the integrity and fairness of the income tax. The approach has been tried so often and failed so often, however, that it is difficult to imagine success after 30 years of failure. It is simply time to try something different. Different approaches may also fail, but we would at least be battling along different lines where vested interests are not so clearly perceived.

Given that America has already moved a long way toward converting the personal income tax into a personal consumption tax we should complete the process. With the establishment and extension of tax-free Individual Retirement Accounts, savings are gradually geing exempted from taxes. Given a national need to raise savings, this process should be encouraged. If the existing IRAs were expanded so that individuals could save any amount of money for any purpose for any period of time without paying taxes except when funds were withdrawn, the present personal income tax would effectively become a personal consumption tax. Any income saved becomes a deduction from taxable income, and, as a result, the income tax would become a tax on consumption (income minus saving).

As long as people were prohibited from moving old funds from taxable to the new tax-free savings accounts, such a change would be an efficient way to stimulate savings. Unless taxpayers were willing to save, there would be no loss of tax revenue. A taxpayer would have to save $3, for example, to gain a $1 tax reduction if he were in the 33 percent income tax bracket. Individuals would end up paying taxes on their income up to the amount that was consumed. If they earned, say $30,000 and saved $3,000, they would pay taxes on $27,000. Or if they earned $30,000 and borrowed $3,000 for consumption purposes or reduced their tax-free savings account by $3,000, they would pay taxes on $33,000.

Viewed as a consumption tax, only three special provisions should be left in the tax code. Since gifts to charities and state and local taxes are not personal consumption, they should still be deducted from total income to get personal consumption expenditures. Since housing expenditures are partly consumption and partly investment, mortgage-interest deductions should be allowed but restricted to one house and for no more than

$500,000. All other special deductions and credits should be eliminated.

With such a change, some of the special provisions now in the tax code would lose their relevance and political defenders. Lower tax rates for capital gains, for example, are defended on the grounds that they are necessary to stimulate investment. With unlimited tax-free savings this provision would not be necessary since income from the sale of appreciated assets would not be taxed if it were invested in other assets. If consumed, however, it would and should be taxed at normal rates.

In our current income tax, tax rates begin at 12 percent tax on taxable incomes up to $3,400 for married couples and end with a 50 percent tax on income in excess of $85,600. This rate structure should be modified in a number of ways. Personal exemptions should be modified so that they are equal to the poverty lines for families of different sizes. Since the poverty line represents the lowest amount of income a family needs to have an acceptable standard of living in our society, it does not make sense for society to tax income below this level. In 1983 this would mean an exemption of about $10,000 for a family of four.

Under present rates the highest tax payers must earn $1 to have 50 cents in after-tax spendable income. Thus to have an equivalent consumption-tax rate, the marginal tax rate on consumption in excess of $85,600 would have to be 100 percent just to keep the current degree of progressivity. The person at that level of expenditures would have to pay a tax of 50 cents for every 50 cents in spending to be treated exactly as he is now being treated. As a result, marginal tax rates should rise from 12 percent for the first dollar of taxable consumption to 100 percent for consumption of $85,600. But the rate structure should not stop there. In a period of national reconstruction conspicuous consumption should be discouraged. Tax rates should continue to be increased above $85,600 at the rate of 1 percentage point for every $1,000 of extra consumption, so that those consuming $185,600 would pay a marginal tax of 200 percent on consumption, those spending $285,600 would pay a marginal tax of 300 percent, and so on up the conspicuous consumption scale.

A Gasoline Tax

Outside of North America every industrial democracy has a tax on gasoline of more than $1 per gallon. The case for such a tax is simple and compelling. America is a major oil importer with a huge balance-of-payments deficit; militarily it cannot afford to be hostage to the whims of middle eastern politics. Arranging our economy so that we do not need Middle Eastern oil is much easier than protecting a Middle Eastern oil supply which we desperately need. A large gasoline tax which reduced consumption and cut our dependence on world oil supplies would be both cheaper and more effective that the rapid deployment force that we are now planning for the Middle East.

A gasoline tax is also a big revenue raiser and would go a long way toward eliminating the deficit. As a result, we should raise our gasoline tax by $1 per gallon. Such a tax would raise approximately $116 billion.[13]

While the proposed tax changes would come into effect gradually, the effects can be illustrated by looking at 1982 expenditures and taxes. In 1982 the Federal government spent $764 billion and collected $614 bil-

Table 2. Federal Revenue 1982 [14]

	Existing Law	*Proposed Law*
Personal income tax	$297 billion	$ 0 billion
Personal consumption tax	0	424
Personal nontax payments	8	8
Corporate profit tax	46	0
Indirect business taxes	48	31
Social insurance taxes	218	154
Value-added tax	0	325
New gasoline tax	0	116
Total	$614 billion	$1050 billion
Expenditures	$764 billion	$764 billion
Surplus or deficit	−$147 billion	+$286 billion

lion for a deficit of $147 billion (see Table 2). If the personal income tax had been replaced with a personal consumption tax, the corporate income tax eliminated, the payroll tax reduced, a value-added tax established, and a $1 gasoline tax added, the federal government would have had a surplus of $286 billion dollars. In such a system, the United States could afford to enact much lower tax rates in the new system of consumption taxation. The time has come to start over and shift to a new tax system. [15]

I am well aware that none of the tax changes just outlined are politically feasible. They are necessary, however, and the political ground must be prepared to make them politically feasible. For if you ask how we are going to solve our problems within the constraints of current political feasibility, the answer is that we are not going to solve our deficit problems because there are no solutions that lie within the bounds of current political feasibility. Those bounds have to be widened.

Revamping Our Expenditure System

On the expenditure side of the budget the Federal government undertakes a surprisingly limited number of activities. Basically it pays for national defense (32 percent of total spending), pays interest on the national debt (11 percent), writes checks to raise individual incomes (36 percent), and writes checks to state and local governments (11 percent). Housekeeping functions such as the president, the congress, and the courts take 2 percent and everything else—education, training, the weather bureau, the national parks—take only 8 percent of the federal budget (see Table 3).

Interest payments are not controllable in the budget. They are set by the Federal Reserve. The housekeeping functions have to be funded. And "other" activities are both too small to make much differences and vital to the quality of life. In any case, the Reagan administration

Table 3. The Federal Budget 1982[16]

	Dollars (billions)	Percent
Defense, space, foreign affairs veterans	$241[a]	32
Interest payments	85	11
Transfer payments excluding those for defense purposes	278	36
Grant-in-aid to state and local governments	84	11
All other	76	10
Total	$764	100

[a] Includes pensions of retired military personnel and civilian employees of the defense department.

has squeezed all of the blood out of these programs that there is to be squeezed.

Grants in aid to state and local government can easily be cut at the federal level, but we are just kidding ourselves when we do so. For most of the functions have to be done, and cuts in the aid means financing them at the local level.

A cut in grants in aid which shifts the locus of budget deficits from the federal government to state and local governments does not help. A deficit is a deficit and a subtraction from national savings wherever it occurs. The whole issue of federalism and what should be done by whom and who should pay for it needs to be rethought, but a new division of authority is not going to solve the deficit problem. That can only be done by raising taxes or cutting expenditures—not by reshuffling the deficit back and forth between different levels of government.

As a result, if one is talking about cutting the federal budget by any significant amount, one has to talk about defense or transfer payments. Defense is an issue; economics is not, and should not, be paramount. A country decides what is necessary for its defense and then goes about raising and spending those funds in the most efficient possible way.[17]

Given the need to be competitive internationally, however, there are some economic realities that need to be taken into account in defense spending. Defense spending is a form of consumption. Neither an MX missle nor an automobile contributes to our ability to produce more goods and services in the future. As a result, if we need to raise defense spending, any increases in public defense consumption must be paid for by cutting private civilian consumption. If investment spending on people or machines is cut to fund defense spending, one is taking public consumption out of the investment funds necessary to be competitive—and one should not then be surprised if one is then not competitive.[18]

Having essentially taken defense out of investment ever since World War II, the consequences have now caught up with us to produce an uncompetitive economy. If the 8 percent of GNP spent on defense in the United States is compared with the 1 percent of GNP spent on defense in Japan, that 7 percent difference would go a long way toward closing the investment gap between Japan and the United States.

In the 1950s when the U.S. was wealthier than the rest of our allies, it could afford to spend more and from the point of view of equity should have carried more of the burden of allied defense spending. But as foreign per-capita GNPs have caught up or narrowed the gap with the American per-capita GNP, what once was a fair distribution of economic burdens has become unfair. Defense absorbs 8 percent of the GNP, over 30 percent of our technical manpower, and almost 40 percent of our durable-goods production, but its absorption of quality is probably even more important than its absorption of quantity. Defense research by its very nature is exciting scientific research. It is usually closer to the frontiers of what is scientifically possible than civilian research since economic constraints are less binding. New weapons will be built almost regardless of costs, new cars will not.

Suppose a new MIT engineer is offered a job designing a better car and a job building laser space weapons. Which job does he take? To ask the question is to answer it. The laser space weapon is more exciting, and thus the "best and the brightest" are apt to go into military research and development. And when the best of America are working on space weapons while the best of Japan are working on better cars, no one should be surprised that Japanese cars are better than American ones. American missiles are better than the nonexistent Japanese ones, but there is little market for the resulting product.

The quantitative competitive problem is in principle solvable. It is technically feasible for America to spend more on defense than Japan and still have a world-class economy if we are willing to pay for it by raising taxes to cut civilian consumption. The qualitative problem, even in principle, is not so easily solved. If the very best of our resources are in military research and production, the civilian economy is deprived of those resources. To stop this from happening one would have to limit the freedom of our very best technical personal to take what they think are the best jobs open to them, and that we are unlikely to do.

An alliance is by its nature a cooperative relationship. That means agreeing with your allies both as to the nature of the threat and as to the nature of the response. If they cannot be brought around to American views as to the nature of the threat and the amounts that should be spent to counter that threat, then America has to rethink. Perhaps they are right about the nature of the threat. Even if they are not, perhaps we really cannot afford to go it alone and conduct the massive solo buildup in military spending that we now are.

Given its competitive position, America can no longer afford to spend much larger fractions of its GNP on defense than its military allies but economic competitors. The problem is not for them to pay more or for us to pay less but for all of us to agree on what needs to be spent and then to allocate the resulting burdens in ways that correspond to today's realities about ability to pay.

The Elderly

Social-welfare programs immediately conjure up images of vast amounts of money being spent on the poor, but that is not in fact where the money is spent. Middle-class Americans tend to forget that that most social-welfare spending goes to programs designed to keep middle-class Americans from falling out of the middle class when they become ill, elderly, or unemployed.

Three percent of the federal budget goes to unemployment insurance.[19] But with limited coverage (only 40 percent of the unemployed received benefits in 1982) and limited benefits (only 43 percent of weekly wages are replaced), it is clear that unemployment-insurance expenditures are not going to be cut by reducing coverage or benefits even more. The only real cure is a prosperous low-unemployment economy.

Any serious civilian budget cutting has to begin with the problems of the elderly, for in the 1982 fiscal year, 35 percent of the entire federal budget went to help the elderly in the form of pensions, welfare payments, or health care. As is true with military expenditures, America can afford to do what is necessary to keep our elderly (ourselves) from declining into a miserable existence as they (we) grow older.

The right level of expenditures depend upon our views of equity for different generations. How much should children contribute to the support of their parents? How much of a burden should parents impose on their children? For this is what Social Security is all about. Each of us, on average, is basically paying the benefits that go to our own parents; each of us, on average, hopes to get benefits from our children when we are old.

Social Security is the crown jewel of American social

legislation. If it did not exist, it would simply have to be invented. Left alone, may individuals simply will not save enough for their old age, and the rest of us are not willing to see them starve. President Reagan is just wrong when he says, ''I am not sure that the benefits that you will receive when you come to the point of retiring from the work force will justify the amount of that [social-security] tax.'' Social-Security taxes do not disappear. They are paid to our own parents and grandparents. If the system did not exist, each of us would individually have to pay for our own parents or watch them suffer in poverty.

While we have not eliminated poverty among the elderly any more than we have eliminated it among the young, great progress has been made. In 1967 the incidence of poverty among the elderly (29.5 percent) was more than twice that of the entire population (14.2 percent).[20] A just society does not economically discard its citizens simply because they have reached 65 years of age. As a result, Social-Security benefits were expanded to lower the incidence of poverty among the elderly. The programs succeeded. In 1983 the incidence of poverty among the elderly was lower (14.1 percent) than that among the population as a whole (15.2 percent).[21]

Similarly, when Social Security was started there was a wide gap in the living standards of the average elderly person and the rest of the population. In 1982, the per-capita cash household income of the elderly slightly exceed that of the entire population.[22] Since the young pay for their medical care while the elderly enjoy Medicare and since the elderly have more wealth than the young, it is clear that the average elderly family now enjoys a standard of living higher than that of younger people. Much of this progress can be traced to Social Security.

If Social -Security and Medicare were to be abolished, the income of the average elderly family would be more than cut in half. Many elderly families depend entirely on Social Security for their standard of living.

The country should hold a victory celebration. We have created a just society where the elderly are treated as well as the rest of the population. That is something to take pride in. A victory celebration does not, of course, obviate the need to solve the system's financial problems.

Part of the problem is caused not by the elderly but by the performance of the economy. With no growth between the first quarter of 1979 and the first quarter of 1983, tax revenues have not risen as rapidly as expected. A stagnant economy inevitably leads to stagnant Social-Security revenues.

Social Security also suffers from one of those good news-bad news dilemmas. During the 1950s, Americans who reached the age of 65 could expect to live an average of 14.1 additional years.[23] By 1980, a 65 year old could look forward to 16.4 years of life with most of the increase occurring during the period after Medicare came into existence—good news. But an increase in life expectancy of 2.3 years raises system costs by 16 percent since everyone has to be supported for 16.4 and not 14.1 years—bad news.

In the long run, the system also runs into problems after 2012 when the baby-boom generation starts to retire and must be supported by the baby-dearth generation.[24] With more retirees per worker, tax rates would clearly have to rise in a stagnant economy, but the extent of the rise in a dynamic growing economy depends upon how fast real per-capita income (productivity) is rising. If productivity were to rise at a fast enough rate, Social-Security tax rates would not have to rise even were there more retirees relative to the number of workers. As a result, restoring economic prosperity is of relevance not just to the work force but to those in retirement.

One of the ways to create a prosperous economy in the twenty-first century is to build up a surplus in the Social-Security trust funds that can be used now to make the investments that are necessary to re-create prosperity and can then be drawn down to ease the burdens on those who are working and paying Social-Security taxes in the twenty-first century.

In 1982 President Reagan appointed a bipartisan committee that came to be known after its chairman as the Greenspan committee to study how the Social-Security problem should be "solved." In the aftermath of the Greenspan report, Congress decided on higher payroll taxes, a longer delay in cost of living increases, a later retirement age in the twenty-first century, inclusion of new federal employees in the system, and taxes on benefits for high-income retirees making over $32,000 to prevent any Social-Security crises in the next few years. But, long before the twenty-first century rolls around, fundamental reforms will have to be made in Social Security.

As seen in the earlier discussion of payroll taxes, they simply cannot be used to do what is planned. As previously suggested payroll taxes should be reduced by one-third and any growth in Social-Security expenditures should be financed with revenue from the new value-added tax. Such a change has a number of advantages. If a significant fraction of Social-Security spending were financed through a value-added tax, those who save (consumed less) would essentially be able to buy their pension benefits cheaper than those who do not save. By taxing consumption, capital income as well as earnings would effectively be partially taxed. High-income elderly people would also essentially continue paying retirement taxes after they had retired. As a result, the system would end up being much less of a transfer from poor workers to wealthy retirees than it is now. The system would become both more efficient and more equitable.

Given that Social Security is a system of transfers of income from one generation to another (not an insurance system) and given that the income of the elderly now slightly exceeds that of younger people, the time has come to recognize that we are all Americans in the same economic boat, subject to the same economic tides. If the tide is rising more slowly, then the standards of living of the elderly must fall or rise more slowly. The standards of living of the elderly cannot rise while those of the rest of the country fall. That is neither fair nor economically feasible.

Since the average American income is governed by what happens to the per-capita GNP, the standard of living of the elderly should be governed by the same factor. To accomplish this, Social Security benefits should be indexed to the per-capita GNP instead of being tied to the consumer price index and periodic increases in benefits as they now are.

Indexing the system to the per-capita GNP would neither raise nor lower future benefits. It simply makes future benefits contingent on our degree of economic success. If the American economy is very successful over the next few decades, the elderly's real standard or living would rise faster tied to the per-capita GNP that it would rise under the current system. If the American economy fails, then the elderly would get less. In the stagnant economy of the early 1980s, for example, such a change would have meant a July 1982 benefit increase of 4 percent rather than the 7.4 percent actually allowed under the present system.

To do less is to be unfair to the elderly. To do more is to be unfair to the young.

The final problem is that of the retirement age. If Americans are living longer and remaining healthy longer, what was a reasonable retirement age (65) becomes an unreasonable retirement age both in terms of forcing people to retire or in allowing them to retire. While ancient numbers seem to have an instinctive wisdom, a retirement age of 65 is not one of those numbers that have intrinsic wisdom. No one, for example, has ever presented health studies indicating that 65 is the age at which working abilities start to suffer a rapid deterioration.

Bismark is usually given credit for picking 65 as the retirement age, but he actually chose 70 as the minimum retirement age in the first public retirement system in the nineteenth century.[25] The Germans lowered the retirement age to 65 in World War I. With a high retirement age and a short life expectancy what looked like a generous social-welfare system, and what was in fact later to become a generous social-welfare system with longer life expectancy, cost very little at the beginning.

Realistically, as the number of years of life expectancy after age 65 lengthens, the retirement age is going to have to rise. Two factors have to be kept in mind as the retirement age lengthens, however, First, everyone should receive plenty of warning as to when they are going to be allowed (or forced) to retire. Retirement takes planning in terms of being able to provide enough savings to supplement Social Security and have the retirement income that the elderly would like to have. Retirement plans cannot be changed on short notice. As a result everyone should know at least 15 years ahead of time as to what their own retirement age will be.

Given what has been happening to life expectancy at age 65, the currently enacted extensions in the legal retirement age, 66 in 2004 and 67 in 2009, are unlikely to be large enough. Basically, the retirement age should be escalated with life expectancy so that the average person can expect the 16 years of retirement benefits that he or she now enjoys. Based on what has actually happened to life expectancy in the previous decade, the retirement age should be raised with a 15-year lag. Thus, in 1985 we would raise the retirement age in the year 2000 to 67 if life expectancy had risen by two years from 1975 to 1985. Then, in 1995 we would again raise the retirement age in the year 2010 based upon how much life expectancy had gone up between 1985 and 1995.

While changes such as those just suggested for social security do not save any money in the short run, they have a tremendous impact on reducing budgetary pressures in the long run. The goal should not be a year-to-year bandaging of the system, but a major operation that puts the patient on its feet again for another half century. In doing so it is not necessary to cripple or dismantle Social Security. The necessary changes can make it into a better program than it now is.

Health Care

Budgetary policy for health care, or more accurately social policy, must be developed. Health is an area where better policies are necessary not just for the federal budget (Medicare and Medicaid) and not just for state budgets (Medicaid), but also for the private economy (health insurance). Public and private expenditures on health care have risen from 5 to 11 percent of the GNP from 1960 to 1983. Clearly, the country cannot afford to let health-care costs rise at the same rate over the next two decades, but this is precisely where we are headed.

Health-care expenditure problems are created by poorer economic performance, repidly advancing and ever more expensive medical technology, and an inconsistent set of ethical principles. No set of expenditures can forever rise faster than the GNP. There is no magic, precise limit on health-care expenditures, but there is, at the same time, a limit. Every dollar spent on health care is a dollar that cannot be spent on something else. Just as one can go broke buying luxury goods so can one go broke buying health care. At some point spending has to slow down to the rate of growth of GNP. If this did not happen, health expenditures would gradually rise to absorb all of GNP.

In the United States we are reaching this point sooner rather than later because of the economy's poor performance over the past 15 years. If productivity had consistently grown at a 3 percent rate and the economy had consistently been operated at full employment, today's health-care spending would account for only 7 to 8 percent of the GNP, and there would be less pressure to control health-care spending.

The need to restore productivity growth with more investment in physical and human resources means that the growth of something else must be restrained, and health care is a big part of that something else. Rising international competition makes health expenditure reforms almost a necessity. American auto workers, for example, make only slightly more than Japanese workers ($10.27 in Japan and $11.80 in the United States), but fringe benefits expand the difference with total wages rising to $13.50 in Japan and almost $22 in America.[26] At the Chrysler corporation medical care accounts for $2.74 per hour of those fringe benefits. Health care costs are an important part of the competitive problem.

It has been traditional medical practice in the United States to employ treatments until those treatments have no marginal payoff or until the undesirable side effects start to overwhelm the benefits. But with the development of more and more expensive techniques (artificial kidneys, heart transplants, expensive diagnostic machines) that can marginally prolong life, the expenditures that have to be made before this traditional stopping point is reached have grown to almost unlimited levels. If, for example, just one-half of those in their last year of life were to be given an artificial heart, the treatment alone would take one-third of the GNP. As it is, Medicare spends 21 percent of its funds on those in the last six months of their life.[27]

The problem is not wasted expenditures where benefits are zero or negative but cases where there are benefits—the probability of an accurate diagnosis goes up from 97 to 98 percent, the chance of survival rises from 3 to 3.1 percent—but the benefits are very small in relation to the costs.

The development of this new medical technology requires a shift in medical practice. Instead of stopping treatments when benefits cease to exist, treatments must be stopped when marginal benefits are equal to marginal costs. But who is to make this ethical decision and decide where that point lies—the patient, the doctor, some third-party payer? Where lies the point where we can no longer afford a medical treatment that will in fact marginally benefit someone?

All of this leads to an ethical debate and Americans are very uncomfortable having to make ethical decisions. In the past we have simply lived with inconsistent ethical principles. We were simultaneously egalitarians and capitalists. None of us wanted to die because we could not afford to buy existing treatments and few of us want to see others die because they could not afford to buy existing treatments. But we were also capitalists and believed that individuals should be allowed to spend their money on whatever they wished, including health care. This set of beliefs has led to an expensive life-prolonging treatment. Being capitalists the wealthy are allowed to buy the treatment privately and marginally extend their lives. Moderate-income individuals who cannot privately afford the treatment want it. They demand it. And being egalitarians they get it either through private health insurance or public programs.

Being quasiegalitarians, we do not have the political ability to say no to a man dying of a treatable disease on the steps of the Massachusett's state house while some other wealthier man is next door being treated at the Massachusetts General Hospital for the same problem. Being quasi capitalists we also do not have the ability to tell the wealthier man that he cannot spend his own money to save his own life so that we can say no to the man who cannot afford to pay. We have to give the treatment to everyone or deny it for everyone, but we can neither deny it nor afford to give it.

In the summer of 1983 such a situation arose with heart transplants. Regulatory authorities were preventing Massachusetts hospitals from performing heart transplants to save money. Some Massachusetts citizens were able to fly to California to get transplants, others were not, but they needed them just as badly. The media and the public essentially wheeled those needing treatment up on the state house steps and dared the public authorities to let them die for want of treatment. Not surprisingly, the public authorities did not dare to do this. They altered rules and regulations to pay for the California heart transplants and quickly began to allow Massachusetts hospitals to perform heart transplants.

I do not pretend to know whether the costs and benefits of heart transplants have reached the point where Massachusetts hospitals should or should not be allowed to perform them, but I do know that this is the wrong way to make the decision. As medical costs rise, it becomes less and less possible to live with our inconsistent ethical beliefs. At some point, and the point is now, they have to be sorted out. Our traditional answer has been health insurance, but it cannot do what needs to be done. Insurance is an appropriate answer to situations where there is a small probability of a disaster which will incur large fixed loses. Fire insurance is the best example. Only a few of us will be unfortunate enough to have our home burn down and the maximum loss is fixed by the value of our house. As a result, we pool our risks and compensate those who suffer losses. Companies make money by being skillful at estimating risks and choosing who they wish or do not wish to insure.

In contrast, large health expenditures are becoming almost universal. Before they die, everyone will be able to make use of large amounts of health care. In this circumstance, insurance becomes not a pooling of small risks but a distortion of incentives. In any insurance system where costs are being paid rather than previous loses refunded, prices are set below costs as the individual sees it. Each of us makes a lump-sum payment, our insurance premium, and, then, when we use medical care, we are able to buy it below cost. Insurance pays all or part of the bills. This encourages each of us to consume more medical care—on the margin it is cheap—but when we all do so we raise next year's lump-sum payments.

Health insurance creates a problem where the losses are not fixed as they are in the case of the burnt house but elastic depending upon how we plan to treat our ailments. For health insurance, the problem is magnified since each time it is relied upon creates an incentive to take the "don't spare the expenses" route since we are talking about our own life or our own health. Each of us knows that if all of us use a lot more health care, each of us will have to pay higher insurance premiums. However, we also know that our own individual expenditures have essentially no impact on next year's insurance rates. As a result, each of us goes ahead with our "don't spare the expenses" purchases and in the process collectively raise next year's insurance rates by a substantial amount.

The system essentially becomes a pass-through system where the insurance companies are making money not by assessing risks and selecting their potential patients more carefully (we legally insist that everyone have access to health insurance), but by taking a management fee that depends upon total expenditures. In this circumstance the insurance companies have an interest in higher health-care expenditures, doctors have an interest in higher health care expenditures since their incomes go up, and each of us has no interest in restraining our own health care expenditures. The result is not surprisingly a system with exploding expenditures.

The health-care problem is not a federal-budget problem. It is a social problem. The limits are the same regardless of whether the money is spent through the federal budget or private insurance. Somehow we are going to have to learn to say no. One solution is to use the market mechanism, but this is basically to let the capitalistic part of our ethics dominate the egalitarian part. We often talk as if the market mechanism is a mechanism for producing less waste, but that is not its prime virtue. It is a mechanism for saying no, but saying no in a very inegalitarian way. Since the richest 20 percent of all households has 11 times as much income as the poorest 20 percent in the United States, any efficient market mechanism will end up giving 11 times as much care to the top 20 percent as it gives to the bottom 20 percent.

The present proposals of the Reagan administration for higher deductibles and prospective rather than retrospective payment are good examples of the problem. The government announces that Medicare will pay less and users must pay more to discourage use of expensive health-care facilities. Private health-insurance companies quickly announce that they will sell private health insurance to cover what is not covered by the government—thus undercutting the whole purpose of the larger payments by patients. Those with money can afford the coinsurance and do not face the incentives to use less. Those without money cannot afford coinsurance and do face the incentives. But are we really going to say that patients who cannot make the necessary private payments are not going to get medical care when they need it and others are going to get it?

With prospective payment, hospitals are paid based on the disease diagnosed and not on how much it costs to treat the disease. What results? Hospitals require more out-patient tests and procedures to reduce in-patient costs and admit only those patients who are "low-cost" patients in each diagnostic class. Once again this leaves the high cost patients out in the cold.

These patients are then "dumped" as uninsured high-cost patients are now dumped. No hospital wants to treat patients without money, and they are sent on to other hospitals—usually the municipal hospital in big cities. Boston City Hospital reports that it gets an average of four "dumps" per month.[28] It also spends twice as much on charity care ($148 million in 1983) as all of the other hospitals in Boston combined. But as city governments with their own budget problems attempt to restrain municipal hospital expenses, treatment at such hospitals increasingly becomes second-class treatment.

Market mechanisms work when the buyer is knowledgeable or willing to live with mistakes and when society is willing to distribute goods and services in accordance with the market distribution of income. In the case of health care, neither of the two necessary conditions exists. In the process of doing what markets do, market mechanisms also create and alter values. Markets are supposed to encourage firms to segment, cream, and dump markets to seek the most-profitable nitches while ignoring areas of low profitability. To deny that this is what they will do is to deny that markets are efficient. In a market environment doctors and hospitals are income maximizers—nothing more and nothing less. In a market environment subsidies cannot be extracted from the wealthy with minor ailments to help pay for the poor with major ailments.

What the theory of market mechanisms fails to consider is that an egalitarian distribution of health care is one of the factors that creates social solidarity, a feeling of community, and nonmonetary attachments. The theory of market mechanisms are a way to say no if we are willing to live with the consequences.

If you are an egalitarian when it comes to medical care, as I am, what is the answer. One answer is for the third-party payers, the firms who pay 35 percent of all medical bills or the government which pays 27 percent of all medical bills, to write sets of rules and regulations as to what they will or will not pay and to prohibit others from buying what is not allowed under the private or public insurance systems. This is essentially how the British have kept health care spending at half the American levels.[29] Such a procedure works, but it works clumsily since no set of rules can be adjusted to accomodate the differences between individual medical problems. Far better if American doctors would begin to build up a social ethic and behavioral practices to determine when medicine is bad medicine not because it has no payoff or because it hurts the patient but because the costs simply are not justified by the benefits. Social mores can be created. If such mores could be created and then legally defended against malpractice suits, it might be possible to build up a system with doctor-imposed cost controls that would be much better and much more flexible than a system constrained with outside cost controls imposed by the third-party payers. In all likelihood, however, we are going to be moving to a system of third-party controls.

As a society, how much are we willing to spend (willing to sacrifice) on prolonging life? The easy answer is "any amount," but that answer is neither true nor feasible. As a result we are going to have to come to some social consensus as to the trade-off between costs and the life extending benefits that result.

The Bottom Line

Expenditures can be cut. Taxes can be raised. And both can be done in such a way that we have a better society. But to do so requires a political process capable of allocating income reductions across the electorate. Few democratic political processes have proven capable of taking such actions without the help of an external threat.

The next five years will simply be a test of whether we can politically respond to a severe problem that is not a crisis or whether we will let that severe problem fester, creating problems that become harder and harder to solve.

Notes

1. *International Financial Statistics*. (Washington D.C.: International Monetary Fund, March 1984), pp. 460, 254, 196, 264, 188, 130, 454.

2. *Economic Report of the President* (Washington D.C.: Council of Economic Advisers, 1984), pp. 220 and 250.

3. Ibid., pp. 250 and 220.

4. Ibid.

5. *Economic Report of the President*, op. cit., p. 251.

6. Ibid., p. 308.

7. Allen Sinai and Otto Eckstein, "Tax Policy and Business Fixed Investment Revisted" (Washington, D.C.: Office of Tax Analysis, April 1981), pp. 1–35.

8. *Economic Report of the President*, 1984, op. cit.

9. Based on Data Resources GNP projection for 1984. *The Data Resources Review* Nov. 1984 (Lexington, Mass: Data Resources, Inc.), p. 1.

10. Joseph A. Peckman and Benjamin A. Okner, *Who Bears the Tax Burden?* (Washington, D.C.: The Brookings Institution), 1974.

11. Senate Committee on the Budget, *Tax Expenditures* (Washington, D.C.: U.S. Government Printing Office, September, 1978).

12. *Estimates of Income Unreported on Individual Income Tax Returns.* Publication 1104(9-79) (Washington, D.C.: Internal Revenue Service, 1983).

13. *Survey of Current Business* (Washington, D.C.: U.S. Department of Commerce, July 1983), pp. S-27, S-28.

14. Ibid., p. 53.

15. Melissa Brown, *Tax Choices* (Washington, D.C.: Roosevelt Center for American Policy Studies, 1983). Joseph A. Pechman, *Tax Policies for the 1980s* (Washington, D.C.: The Brookings Institution, 1982). Charles R. Hulten and June O'Neill, "Tax Policy," *Changing Domestic Priorities* (Washington, D.C.: The Urban Institute, 1982).

16. *Survey of Current Business,* op. cit., p. 53.

17. *Rethinking Defense and Conventional Forces:* Alternatives for the 1980s # 8. (Washington, D. C.: Center for National Policy, 1983). Staff of Joint Economic Committee, "The Defense Buildup and the Economy" (Washington, D.C.: Staff of the Joint Economic Committee, 1982).

18. Charles L. Schultze, "Economic Effects of the Defense Budget" *The Brookings Bulletin,* (Washington, D. C.: The Brookings Institution, Fall 1981), p. 2.

19. *Survey of Current Business,* op. cit., p. 53.

20. *Money Income and Poverty Status of Families and Persons in the United States,* 1982. Series P-60 # 124 (Washington, D.C.: Bureau of the Census, 1983), p. 21.

21. Ibid.

22. Ibid, p. 19.

23. *Statistical Abstract of the United States,* 1982–83 (Washington, D. C.: U.S. Department of the Commerce), p. 71.

24. Peter A. Morrison, "Demographic Links to Social Security," *Challenge,* vol 26, no. 1 (Jan/Feb 1982), p. 44.

25. Robert J. Myers, "Bismark Backed 70," *Wall Street Journal* (November 7, 1977), p. 19.

26. "Wage Questions," *New York Times,* (May 13, 1983), p. D3; "Chrysler Hurt by Costs," *New York Times* (March 5, 1984), p. B8.

27. *Health Care Financing* (Washington, D.C.: U.S. Department of Health and Human Services), p. 1.

28. Richard A. Knox, ''Some Local Hospitals 'Dump' the Uninsured,'' *Boston Globe* (February 6, 1984), p. 31.

29. Henry J. Aaron and William B. Schwartz, *The Painful Prescription* (Washington, D. C.: The Brookings Institution, 1984). *Health Vote 1982* (Washington, D. C.: Public Agenda Foundation, 1983).